THE ORACLE WITHIN

Living the Intuitive Life

BY

JENNIFER POSADA

THE ORACLE WITHIN

ISBN: 9781931032988
Library of Congress Catalog Card Number: 2006907125

For Sebastian,
for the little girl who believed,
for the Oracles of all times,
and for you,
the Ones who Remember.

Contents

Preface

I would like to tell you, before we begin, that I have not written this book by the rules of convention. I have written this book by the voice of my heart.

I believed that I could make my book readable and enjoyable, and still be true to myself. I knew that the writing and the message would be more powerful that way, and more full of my intention in expressing them.

I haven't used semi-colons, have used run-on and incomplete sentences, and capitalized inconsistently. However, I did it all with purpose. For instance, sometimes capitalizing a word gives it a connotation or emphasis I did not want it to have every time. Sometimes it distracts from the meaning of the phrase, or even of the word itself. Alternately, sometimes I did want to give that emphasis to a word not usually capitalized.

You see, I wrote as if I were speaking this book, or even as if it were a poem. May it touch your heart and change your life, as everything within it has so much changed mine. May love follow close to you every day of your life, and forever beyond.

When the first sunlight shone on my hand,

I was glad to be in this land,

When I was just a baby,

My heart began to pound,

When the first sunlight shone on my soul,

I love my Self, I said,

When the first sunlight shone on my soul.

My Song, Written age 8

Introduction

Remembering Everything

I can't tell you how it began, because it can't be described in words, but I remember everything.

I remember our origins, and even our futures. My own, and everyone's. I remember as the collective remembers. And so do you, at a level you may not be aware of yet.

I first heard the word Oracle when I was seven years old, but this story begins much earlier. The spark of the light within me did not ignite at some point in my childhood, or become integrated through years of work…it was with me from birth and before. As it is with you. What made me different, which it would take me some time to discover, was that I *remembered.*

Before I could speak, before I could even open my eyes, I knew I was made of God. I knew that everything in this world and any other was made of this divinity, and that therefore

everything inside me was as well. This simple understanding is
the root point of my being from which everything else in my
life has grown. When we discover this is our source, fully and
completely, the fruits of our lives change forever.

In reading my story and the rest of this book you will
find many signs and reminders, like gleaming jewels beside
the path, that lead you back to your own deepest knowledge
of yourself. There are infinite ways to be reminded of your
true nature, and to keep yourself reminded of it daily, so that
you can live within awareness of it. This is the life of miracles
we hear about. I know, because this is the life I lead.

The real work has been done. You have been doing it for
a long time. When you come to the time of remembering
you have come to the time of sweet relief. It is the ultimate
homecoming, coming home to the true Self. Once the work is
complete, there is simply the discovery that the joys of the new
awareness are at your fingertips…and have been placed there
for you to enjoy to the fullest.

The intuitive life is not one we must build up to, but one
we are reduced to when all the other layers of imposed being
have been washed away. It is not a life that we attain by follow-
ing a set of rules, but one which finds us, sometimes when we
are most on our knees and have the fewest answers. It comes
by surrender rather than action. And yet, we can make way for
surrender…we can prepare the space for it to enter our lives
more easily.

The intuitive life is one in which we feel continually connected to the divine source. It is a life in which we are at one with our true nature as it is in each moment, and a life in which we are in love with ourselves in the deepest possible way. It is a life in which we feel intimate with ourselves, and the divine, and therefore invite the most profound intimacy into our lives.

The intuitive life is one of constant affirmation and support. We do not feel alone, even with our challenges, and even the heaviest burdens feel as if they are shared with energies that are strong enough to dissolve them with ease.

Being an Oracle is not just about being psychic, or giving prophecies, it is about having a touchstone in your heart connected to the center of the universe, that you can always go to. At any time of the day or night, in any condition, in any place. It is a gift we all have access to, it just requires remembering that we have it.

We do not heal, we remember the healed state. We do not grow, we remember a different possibility. We do not change, we remember a new future. It is all already within us as potentiality, whether past or future, we are simply being called back or forward to our organic nature and remembering its essence. That nature is the palate of our lives and of our souls, from which masterpieces can be created. Especially once we realize that the brush is in our hands and the colors are infinite.

The intuitive life is not something we have to strive and reach for, trying to draw in, but something we allow to emerge that is already within us. Something we remember how to access, something that is always there.

We have the entire universe inside of us. Not just a fragment.

In the intuitive life we don't lose our fragments, we just know how to welcome them as part of our whole. We still fall into holes, we just have better ropes to pull ourselves out. We still cry, we just don't feel that we are crying alone, and we find a deep, ultimate consolation and source of hope to bridge us to another land.

There is a map inside of you that can lead you anywhere in the universe. If we feel comfortable stretching beyond our usual limits, we can follow these lines of light on a more deeply familiar path. We can see all the things we are looking for, and still walk and interact as humans on this earth. That map of light can be laid over our lives every day, helping us feel which direction is right for us in each moment, illuminating our freedom to choose.

It is no more than the voice of the heart, and our learning to become the instruments and the melody of its music. Therein lies the eternal harmony.

My Story

Finding the Oracle Within

I was born different, but I didn't know it then. I was born remembering.

I was conceived within the Void, and I just never left. Perhaps they didn't give me the forgetting pill, or I slipped through a crack in time, but the essence of "all that is" has been with me, holding me lovingly, forever. I remember.

It makes me no more or less special than anyone or anything. We all remember at our core, and some of us do so very consciously, as I do. For years I did not tell my story, so as not to set myself apart, but it would be an injustice to life for a singing Oracle not to open her mouth or to do so with half-truth.

I am telling my story for the others like me. Like you. I am telling this story for the other ones who wonder if the answers and the power to heal can really be as simple as a moan, or a sigh, or a chance taken on total faith. A free fall from struggle into paradise with one great blind spot in between and nothing but trust to guide the way.

When I was seven my life changed. Sure, there were many signs before then. I knew inexplicably and completely that I came from love, and that the most important thing I could do was to love myself. I knew that if I loved myself I could love all, and I could remember my home and my true nature. I knew this love was the nature of all things, disguised or not, and I knew that what I was made of was holy. This has been the distinguishing mark of my life.

As soon as I learned how to write, I would write myself notes with pictures that read, "I love my Self." Over and over. For me it was the greatest celebration of life.

From my earliest years I could see colors when I closed my eyes, and I knew they were related to people and what they meant. I also could remember some of my past lives.

I would see the "brown spots" in peoples' auras and ask politely if I could remove them and send the green healing energy in their place. If I wanted to know my own colors I could flick open my hands and see which ones were in my field. My mother began to let me choose the babysitters each time based on what I could sense from a distance about their "colors" at the moment. I would tell her not to call a specific one because she was angry, in a bad mood, or getting sick that day.

When I was seven, however, a strange thing happened. As so often occurs in our world, a simple event opened my perception of reality vastly, and other dimensions beckoned again, and welcomed me in.

When I was seven they wheeled me into an operating room and gave me a sock doll to replace my mother, and as our hands were pulled apart in the movement I knew deep within myself that I would never be the same, that somehow in the simple procedure of having my tonsils removed, I was opening a gateway even more deeply to a world I would never again be without.

As the anesthetic took hold I watched the faces of the nurses at the sides of the bed blur into oblivion and their voices fade away from my reach. "Good girl," they said. "You're such a good girl."

My inner vision opened and I saw a three-dimensional graphic image of my head, rotating around and around into space. And then nothing.

When I woke there were no words, just a roughness I could not explain. The sock doll was gone. I needed water, but as hard as I tried I could not speak. Finally a nurse must have heard my whispers and come to me, and someone, at some point must have realized that the simple surgery had been more than that for me. A fight with his wife had left the doctor frustrated, and it had translated into him clamping my jaw open too wide and a carelessness with his work. It was decided that I would stay a couple of nights there in the hospital, instead of returning home that day as planned.

I got the snoopy room. I shared it with a very nice girl my age with red curly hair, who was rushed out of the room in a wheelchair one day with tubes coming from her vagina, and who I never saw again. I have thought about her often, wondering what happened to my strange sister of that experience. Knowing she was never the same either.

It was actually a good psychic friend of my Mother's who told her about the doctor fighting with his wife and his rough treatment as the reason for the complications. So when my Mom called the hospital to discuss it she said to the nurse, "I know about the fight he was having on the phone before the surgery." And before she could contain herself, the nurse confirmed it by responding, "How did you know about that?!"

When I returned home I still had pain in my jaw, and one day as we waited to see yet another physician who might be able to tell us why, I passed out in the waiting room.

I say "passed out" because I don't think it was quite like fainting. A wave would just come over me and surrendering to it always felt like the right decision. Not that I "decided" anything. I just gave over to the wave because I trusted it. I knew its origins were good. Looking back on it, I think about the role the surgery played in my further psychic opening, in that it was my first experience of total anesthesia and had the effect of bringing me in touch with complete surrender, and re-entry into the void.

When I came back I told my mother what was wrong with my jaw, with words beyond my knowledge, and that nothing could be done about it at the time. When the doctor came in and repeated my exact message my mother was floored, and I began my earliest questions about the origin of what had become knowledge that I had never learned. I would come to know that nothing is learned, only remembered.

It is remembered because it is all part of one whole, and as we remember, those parts become the whole again—to remember is to re-member.

I began to pass out regularly. At the drop of a hat really. While walking or sitting, anywhere at all. Always coming back with information or messages. I knew when beings were in the room. I could talk to them. There were scary ones too…that drew near to my light and tried to steal a little piece, but I knew how to turn the light on or call someone near to send them away. I knew they couldn't really get me.

I trusted, but I doubted too. I began to hear about metaphysics through my Mother who, blessedly, had become more deeply involved in such information. I began to wonder what part of my experiences was imaginary. So well taught I was that imagination was not to be confused with reality. So well taught we all are.

You see, I didn't leave my body with a heavy breath like the other channels I heard about…I didn't see the auras with my eyes open. Everything happened inside me, transferable only with imagination onto our fleeting and fascinating physical world.

I was a child. Aside from visiting with the nice beings and warding off the less enlightened ones, I had very little to relate my experiences to, and mine didn't sound like anyone else's I heard about.

One evening my Mother went to see the presentation of a woman who channeled a being named Emmanuel. It was a period of question and answer with the woman, before the channeling had even begun, and my Mother raised her hand to ask a question. She wanted to ask about my "passing out" but all she got out was, "My daughter has been…" when the woman stood up and said, "Emmanuel wishes to speak with you."

When Emmanuel entered he told my Mother, "Your daughter is an Oracle, and we do not send many at this time. Do you remember the bargain that you made this entity?" My Mother gestured that she did not. She says he went on for several minutes with poetic words about our agreement. He told her that she had agreed to love me, but not so much that others could not love me. To support me, but not so much as to stifle me. To push me, but not so hard that I could not move at my own pace. To shepherd me, but not so much as to constrict me. He said she had agreed to write down my words and my wisdom so they could be shared with the world. (I believe we renegotiated that part of the contract, since I decided to write them myself!)

It is important for me to share that I don't believe that those first words of Emmanuel's meant that not many Oracles are present among us, as we are all Oracles within ourselves. I think he meant fully awake Oracles, that came in remembering their past and gifts so early in life.

When my Mother got home that night, bewildered and excited at what she had heard, it was dark and I was sleeping soundly in the hum of ventilated air and the singing of crickets. I was still seven years old at the time, living in the suburbs of Washington DC.

"Jenni"...

I woke to her dim outline sitting on the bed next to me. "Jenni, can you pass out on purpose?"

I didn't think very hard about it. "I don't know," I said. "I'll try." I just sat up in bed and then let myself fall back again. Thinking back on it now I realize that the passing out was a vehicle for surrender, which has been so important to the experience of receiving Oracular guidance for many ages.

I was immediately immersed in the familiar space of the void, and then from that space I suddenly found myself entering a library, a room where the books were shelved to the ceiling, and thick with information. Somehow, instantly, I knew without even exploring that these infinite rooms held all the knowledge in the universe, and that visiting this place I had access to it all. My mind and soul were overcome with the scope and beauty, and humbled by the possibilities.

I immediately wondered what gave me this access, and then quickly knew that we all have it. This "library" is stored in every cell, in every atom, in every particle of creation. It is public domain, and yet only those humble enough to wonder how to respect this gift gain entry. You don't have to know how, you just have to ask.

This event changed my life once again. I had touched eternity in a new way, like having found another well we can draw from to nourish our every-day lives that never runs dry. It is not the "information" in these "books" that brings the ecstasy…it is the memory.

For in a way, as I said before, all healing is memory. Memory of the healed state. That is why reminders are so powerful. The library reminded me of infinity, and that the universe was loving enough to record every moment of existence like an excited mother filling her baby book with every detail of her child.

My mother, however, wanted to talk to a being. So I grabbed the nearest one.

"Is anyone there?" she asked, and I told her there was. She asked who the being was and he said that he was a librarian.

She was deeply disappointed…having hoped for a doctor or holy person of some kind.

She regained her composure, and, trying to make conversation, asked, "So, what kind of books do you tend to?"

"My Dear Woman, I am a keeper of all books both written and unwritten. I am a librarian at the library which contains all the information in the Universe," the being responded.

My mother had gotten more than she had hoped for, and one little girl had glimpsed a reality far beyond her human years. For we are all only partly of this world, though at best completely present in it.

My Mother also took me to a Healer from Poland who had magical hands and a beautiful presence. Though his method did not involve touch, I could always tell where his hands were over my body with my eyes closed, so powerful was his work. In those few sessions, I felt that I was among kindred spirits. I felt validated in my understanding of the subtle realms, and deeply comforted.

The summer of my eighth year, not long after this time, my Mother was out of town at a conference and someone mentioned the name of an island off the opposite coast of our country, and bells went off in her ears. I will always be grateful that they did.

She decided to make a trip to this island, then to the Southwest to see a friend and maybe to stay there, or return at some point to live. So she bought a camper van and put my six-year-old sister Adrianne and me in it, and drove us across the country that summer. We zig-zagged our way through about twenty-five states on our way to the West Coast and saw many magnificent places, securing my love of travel for a lifetime. We camped and ate in our little van, and met characters, and fell in love with landscapes along the way.

But nothing, nothing could have prepared me for finding my home on that little island. I had thought that such beauty and peace only existed in heaven. We stayed there for two weeks, camping, and though we all fell in love with it, we thought we would finish our journey before deciding where we really belonged. We cried leaving on the ferry. However, my Mother had also decided that we would stay wherever the van engine blew, if it did, and when it blew heading up Mount Rainier shortly after leaving our island, she decided it was close enough, and we went back to stay. That was twenty years ago this summer.

We slept on the floor of the home belonging to a woman we had met during our visit, and a couple of days later I started third grade in the local school. Every summer until I finished high-school I would go back to Virginia to visit my Dad, and that same little room that had been mine and never changed as I grew up. When the house was sold, it was those same little toys I had had as a child that were only then finally shifted in the move. For those years it was a time capsule of my early childhood.

And so from that time on, this little island kept me, as her secret, so that I could grow up protected and surrounded by the purest elements of this precious Earth. This island lifted me from the swingsets of the neighborhoods of the suburbs, and enfolded me in her arms so that I could see my reflection all around me at all times…so that I would not get confused.

On this island I could talk to the forests and lose myself in pebbled beaches without any fear of getting lost.

One day I told my Mother that I was seeing something in her friend's aura. She arranged for me to meet with her and tell her about it. When I entered the woman's office, she says I walked around and looked at things, ran my finger along the edge of her desk, and proceeded to tell her with great lucidity that when she was around her boyfriend her aura became black. She tells me that she was greatly impacted by what I shared, and that it rang true to her.

I believe this was how I started giving readings as a little girl. Perhaps I invited her over to tell her more, because at some point around that time my Mother says that she was surprised to find that very same friend dropping by unannounced one day. Though her arrival was unexpected she was glad to see her, and invited her in to share some tea. Her friend responded that she was not there to socialize, but to see me. My Mother watched with an open mouth as I greeted her, took her into my Mother's office and closed the door. A few minutes later I came out saying that I needed a candle, and went back in.

When my Mother's friend left she was dabbing her eyes, and my Mother again asked if they could have tea. "No," she replied, "I need to go home and think." My mother waited until she was gone and asked me right away, "So…what happened? Tell me all about it." She says that I looked at her and said, "Oh no, I could never divulge what happens in a private session!"

After that I began to give readings to my mother's friends, for whom I would answer questions, see energies, offer healing, tell stories, and sing healing songs. I would light a candle and open my box of stones from the beach, crystals, and shells and play them to the music I heard inside, singing the song that person needed to hear to heal, making up words as I went. This old rosewood box and its contents were all deeply meaningful to me, and opening it was like laying out a most sacred altar.

I always liked to have a candle, and even remember a story I told about it. It was one of those pillar candles, about six or eight inches tall, and green. When it was lit, there was a dark portion at the bottom and a more translucent area at the top illuminated by the flame. I told the story of a people who lived at the bottom of the candle, in the dark. They stayed there because they did not believe there was anything else to choose. There were ancient stories told about a light somewhere above their world, but according to the myths, the only ones who had ever taken the risk of traveling to find it had become trapped in some void and had never been seen again. For this reason people feared enough to never step outside the dark and cold world they existed in.

Then I would tell of the ones who were brave enough to look beyond their world, in spite of fear. The ones who climbed the steep slope up onto the edge of the candle, where they could see the flame. When they reached that point they always had two choices. One was to advance slowly and fearfully toward the great, blazing light at the center, and the other was to leap into it. In my story, those that advanced slowly with fear would become trapped by slow movement in the wax. Those that leapt into the light would enter into another world, entirely liberated from the one they had known. I would encourage the person I told the story to have the bravery to travel to the light, and to have faith and jump right into it when they found it.

During all of third grade I wore a flannel bag around my neck full of these stones and crystals, worry dolls and little books of Chinese wisdom and New Age phrases.

I didn't have many friends, which might almost go without saying. The other girls in my cabin laughed at me quite a bit when I brought my crystals to summer camp with me. I wasn't like most of my fellow third-graders. My only friend was the girl with crossed eyes…we were both different.

I was teased for years for being different, and then one year everything different about me became "cool," but of course by then I didn't care. I was looking for real companionship, and though it would take years I would eventually find it.

I had so much in third grade to make up for it all though. I had beings and could read the meanings in the stones. I could feel the animal spirits around us and started writing my own poems about life, filling a book with them and with colored pictures of light and sound. I knew how to use crystals to heal and could see people's colors. Friends would come later, because I had a friend in my Self.

One day I took my mother down to the beach and told her I wasn't going to do any more readings for a while. I told her that I would still have my gifts inside, but that I needed to learn more about how to best give them in this world. When she worried that I might not be able to get my gifts back later, I remember telling her not to be concerned, that I could turn my gifts on and off like flipping a light switch.

Even after that time I would still be in touch with them. I learned Reiki at ten years old, and feeling the flow of energy through my hands wondered how this was different from the innate sense of healing that we all have so instinctually. It would feel like something I not only already knew and practiced often, but that was as familiar as a very old friend, and as fundamental to the soul as sleeping or breathing is to the body.

In my early twenties, a man that I had known briefly when I was little came into a store I was working in. When I recognized him and told him who I was, he became wide-eyed and told me the story of how I healed his foot. He said that he had broken some bones in his foot on a day when he happened to be visiting our house. He made sure I knew that he could tell when he had a broken bone, saying he had broken many in his life. He said that he had asked me to soak it in a bucket with epsom salts, as I was the only one at home, and that I had asked him if I could heal it for him. When he said yes, he says that I put my hands on his foot under the water, and that when he took it out a few minutes later it was completely healed.

Even with my experience as an Oracle I felt that maybe he was exaggerating, so when he told me this I thanked him shyly, but he noticed right away that I had not fully understood him. He grabbed my hand and looked me hard in the eyes and told me again, with even more emphasis, that he knew I had healed his broken bones. I received him more seriously, and thanked him for telling me, and have never seen him again. I tell this part of the story as a reminder that spontaneous healing is not only possible, but a part of our natural abilities.

Almost twenty years after talking to my Mother on the beach that day, I would offer my first reading again. By then I would have traveled to Egypt, Europe, Peru, and India, experiencing music, dance, ancient temples and living saints. Not only in the form of revered masters, but in the loving kindness that is often unnoticed by the masses. I would find these saints bent over one-burner stoves and laundry buckets…sitting on porches and under trees, offering simple graciousness as the only sign of their mastery.

I would seek teachers and shamans who wanted to teach me anything about sound. Exploring new frameworks for the

essential knowingness which had patiently been rapping at my
door my entire human life, waiting over and over again to be
welcomed in by the fire of my self-love.

Knowing that all the answers lie within is no deterrent from
finding new ways to experience them and see them reflected
in the shine of another eye, spoken through the translation of
another soul's version of the great story. They are all so beautiful.

Finally, weary from the great world, my island brought me
back and wrapped me up in its arms, and I began to do my
work again. Now, at the age of twenty-eight, I sit here writing
this book to fulfill a great prophecy, not just one in my own
life, but to speak of one even grander, and more far reaching. I
come as a beacon of the Great Remembering. I come to be the
bearer of the glad tidings of the coming home. I again raise my
shells in song, to call out to the others. To call out to you.

A History of Oracles

When the story began we were all Oracles, not just in potential but in actuality. We all remembered. After all, we had all just been born of bliss quite recently, and it was fresh in our consciousness.

Some of my earliest memories as a Soul took place when the Earth was not yet solid, but still existed in a subtle form. Its form was still experimental. These are my most ancient memories of a land we now call Egypt. It was not really a location then so much as a place in consciousness, a place from which some of us remember dreaming the Earth into being. Walls and objects were not solid, and yet they were visible in some way. All things were translucent. You could read information in space, like a great invisible scroll which rolled out and contained wordless messages that could be understood. This place existed in the realm of potential rather than in the realm of material, though they are inherently unified. Nothing was forgotten then, and nothing felt separate from the whole. We were all one being working as unique aspects, and we were conscious of it.

At some point the dream and the potential birthed form. We didn't know if we were ready, but there was no way to be ready…only the willingness to try and to see what would happen. That event of form birthing from potential began a great journey that we are watching come full circle now.

Some of us knew from the beginning about the Great Forgetting, but not most. You see, we would all begin embodying with full memory and bliss, living in harmonious communities and at one with the divine. Doubt was like a plant that came up in the garden that no one had intended to seed. It just grew. Along with the knowingness of divinity came the duality of doubting it, the desire to question it.

Many people have asked me why this happened. Why, when we had perfect harmony and bliss, did we collectively forget. Many people think this was some great error, but looking deeper at the roots we find that there is a perfect plan even to the Great Forgetting. We see that there are fruits from the journey of forgetfulness to memory, that we will only truly taste as we complete it. There is a great wisdom, like the wisdom of a tree that dies to make room for others to grow. Like the wisdom of a broken heart that opens more deeply in the process of breaking.

When the forgetting began, like seeds of doubt spreading by wind, there were entire communities who knew nothing about it. Then, one day a traveler, a pilgrim of the soul, would come on a journey from somewhere else, in search of something she or he couldn't quite place. They would talk about the ways that things had changed where they had come from...a coldness growing in the hearts of the people. This pilgrim would have a sense that there had once been a greater order, a prevailing truth, but could not quite remember it, like a tune to a once-loved song almost grasped but not quite recalled in the back of one's mind.

The ones who remembered would remind the pilgrim, and she or he would return to their community to remind the others again, and so the Oracles were born. They were simply the ones who still remembered. The ones who remembered where we come from and what we are made of. Love.

When the doubt and the forgetting became epidemic, the Oracles became few, and they themselves needed to be reminded by nature, and by the earth...the greatest Oracles of all. Nature and the earth have never forgotten, and they would remind the ones who agreed to stay conscious and awake, in a world that fell asleep.

Over time the Ones who Remembered became the priestesses and priests, the holy ones and the mystics. They could still talk to the Goddess and to God...to the deities and the Ancient Ones. And the ways of life once common to all became the old ways. The Oracles became the record keepers, remembering the oldest stories, and the most ancient songs of the universe. They remembered love.

Institutions were built around the places where the Oracles could most clearly hear the voices of the earth, nature, and the deities. Temples to the earth goddess became temples to the gods, and then churches when the Oracles were gone.

Ceremonies were invented to store the memory and to make it repeatable. They were created both to celebrate and to teach others who would be born into the world with the destiny of remembering, birth after birth. The ceremonies would help them recall what their souls knew already. At that time each ceremony had a certain framework, but improvisation and creativity were important and cherished parts of the experience. A ceremony only repeated exactly as one had learned it was considered dead, devoid of life and spirit.

Soon the pilgrims came in numbers to the temples. They yearned to remember, for it instantly eased the pain of forgetting which spread like a wildfire over everything in their lives. Life became heavy and full of suffering and despair. They longed to remember the goddess holding open her hands to them and raining blessings into their hearts.

As long as people wanted to remember, the Oracles were honored. They lived in peace and comfort, close to the earth. They wore simple but beautiful fabrics, adorned themselves with leaves and flowers, and walked barefooted on the ground. They spent hours by the ocean and the trees, hearing the voice of the universe singing to them, reminding them of the ultimate truth of our source, and our home.

People brought offerings of foods and goods, and the temples were always well-kept as beautiful houses of the reflection of our true birthplace. They amplified the sound and channeled the light. They were extensions of and celebrations of nature, and of the soul. They were a mirror of that oneness.

And then, very slowly, the people stopped wanting to truly remember. They only came to ask the Oracles if their crops were going to bring a better harvest than their neighbor's, or whether their spouse had been unfaithful to them. The second wave of the Great Forgetting also brought a lust for power as a replacement for remembering, and the ones who sought to gain by creating an illusion of more importance decided that the Oracles and the temples were a source place of that power. They decided that if they could harness it, they could control the people and seal their recognition through falsehood and possession.

This is when the hierarchies began within the communities of those who remembered. This is when the voice of the Oracle could only be translated through a certain few, and then could only be offered to a certain few. The truth of our origins and the ability to tap into the knowledge of the universe became a privilege of only those who had accepted the false power, and the chain of memory began to break at an even deeper level.

By this time the people had not only accepted leaders, they needed them. They did not consult oracles any longer, but authorities and books. Science was the new oracle, and its truth half-lost in "knowledge." Imagination was relegated to child's play and intuition to witchcraft, a legacy that still plays out in our mass consciousness today.

But the Ones who Remembered knew about the Great Forgetting at some point, and of its purpose, and laid down their robes and their sacred items. And, when they lay themselves down to the earth for that last time, they knew they would be forgetting for a while, but not forever. They knew that the memory would be stored in the time capsule of their hearts to reopen when the world was ready to remember, like the village that also slept while sleeping beauty awaited her kiss, so that when she woke it would be as if it had never happened at all.

Only in this case it won't feel that way. It will feel as if it did happen, but none of the suffering will remain…only the fruits of the harvest that can only ripen in darkness. Just as we all began in a darkness made of pure love. There is another darkness though, the mythical one of our greatest fears. That is the darkness of oblivion, a place where we go when we feel truly separate from that pure love. A place where we imagine we are isolated and estranged from any memory of our origin, and it is from that place that we see horrible things come into our world.

The truth is that it is an imaginary place, through real things have happened as a result of the fear of its reality. You see, nothing can be separate from the pure love, because it is everything. This is the revelation of the re-awakening. This is how important your remembering is.

For just as we were the last to sleep, we are the first who awaken and again serve to remind others at this very important time, just as we did so long ago. Our earlier efforts were not in vain, for they set the stage for many of the unfoldments we will experience now. It is the ones who remembered then, the Oracles, who I am calling to as I write these words.

This is the book I was born to write. I was one of those who stayed up all through the night, to be ready, at the agreed upon time, to awaken the other Oracles again, so that we could spread around the Earth and remind all the others one more time.

They will come. They will want to remember. We won't have to open a fissure in the earth to sit over or look into crystal balls. There are very few temples left, but we will make new ones. This time we may share our visions by way of simple compliments or warm connections. No way of sharing love is too small. And we shall have back our beloved communities and our hours of sharing conversation with the trees.

We shall crack the ancient wall of forgetting, for the power of our memory is the strongest force in our world and will crumble the structures of doubt with ease. Simply because it is time. We must remember now or give up on the experiment we dreamed into being in the beginning, when all was still subtle and nothing had yet taken form...when we began to wonder what experiences we might have in density, how we might get home again, and what we might bring back with us upon our return.

Avalon

Do you remember when we circled the fire?
Do you remember nature's empire?
When we closed our eyes to the waking world,
and we entered the place where the mists swirled.

Oh Avalon, I remember you…Oh Avalon, I remember you.

Do you remember when the Goddess was alive,
and how in our hands her grace would arrive?
How on a walk in the woods you were never alone,
and close to the land you always knew you were home.

Oh Avalon, I remember you…Oh Avalon, I remember you.

Do you remember where we met by the well,
where the stories were told and the power would swell?
Where we kneeled to say prayers that were never spoken,
in a land where the promise would never be broken.

Oh Avalon, I remember you…Oh Avalon, I remember you.

Do you remember in the final hour,
how the time had come and we gave up our powers?
How we laid down the stones and the robes were burned,
until the day would come when we swore we'd return…

Oh Avalon, I remember you…Oh Avalon, I remember you.

Do you remember how we circled the fire?

Song by: Jennifer Luna Posada

LIVING
THE INTUITIVE LIFE

THE ORACLE WITHIN

Self-Love

The Sacred Mirror

If I were asked about the purpose of life, this Oracle would say it is to find self-love. And if I could name my greatest gift, it would be that I came here knowing self-love. For it is the gift of self-love that has brought me all others.

Hearing my story or experiencing my work, many have thought my gifts have to do with my ability to see visions, talk to beings, or use my voice to support healing, but I believe they are wrong. The essence of my most profound gift in this world is that I remember the nature of the universe, and in doing so, it is impossible not to love myself as the most intimate part of it. This love has filled my life with abundance of all kinds.

The fact that I have always loved myself doesn't mean I haven't ever doubted, or felt ugly or ashamed. Two very different feelings or self-images can co-exist as we evolve and transform. It just means that all the while I had a guiding light, like a lighthouse I could focus on in stormy black seas. This light has been all the comfort I could hope for, and the answer to every one of my most fervent prayers.

When we have discovered the secret of self-love, it is as if we turn a key in the great door of the universe and all the other mysteries spill out at our feet, suddenly revealed. Discovering self-love is like finding a simple-looking faded paper, that when held up to the light becomes golden, and reveals the true nature of all things. When we love ourselves we know we deserve to feel relief, joy, and even bliss, simply as a part of existing, and we are suddenly so much more free to allow our daily reality to change in whatever ways reflect this knowingness.

Self-love begins with the Void. The Void when described as the place where all things exist in potential, yet nothing is manifest materially. It is the darkness which gives birth to all, the blackness that holds all colors, all lights, all things that have ever been or may ever be. It is the birthplace of us all, and it is one-hundred-percent pure love. It is an endless field of resonant, vibrating love. It is from this, the universe in constant lovemaking with itself, that we and all things are born. We are not just children of the Void however, we *are* the Void. We and the creative principle of the universe are one.

We are both one with everything, and yet each of us is entirely unique. This is what our souls are made up of. We are each our own distinct vibration in a sea of loving oneness. We can merge completely with this oneness, and weave back into

THE ORACLE WITHIN

enjoying our uniqueness like a never-ending, ecstatic dance. We come here to remember that this is all we are supposed to know how to do. The rest is a growth challenge, something to rub up against until we are free. Life is a long succession of finding freedom, and if we don't find it by choosing it in life, we will find it in death and keep trying life after life until we do. Though the karmic wheel is slowing for many of us, and we are moving on from the cycle of evolving by way of reincarnation as we have known it.

It sounds huge, but it starts as simply as not being so hard on yourself. It really is that easy to begin with. When you feel that you have done something wrong, or less than perfectly, or less well than someone else, or with less effort than you could have done it, or without heart or compassion, just acknowledge it and move on. If we could just begin with that most simple of steps we would unravel into self-love pretty quickly.

If we only find beauty in the qualities of others, we must remember that what allows us to observe and appreciate that beauty is that we have it within us. We would otherwise not be able to recognize and value it. Whatever you may love or esteem in others, remember it is actually within you, waiting to be reprojected back inward. When we have projected our beauty onto others, we find it very hard to draw from the well of self-love. We must first reclaim what we have been giving away.

Often we are taught to just pile on the self-judgments and keep moving until we have the proper time to deal with

33

them. By the time we try, because something in our lives has confronted us so deeply that we have no choice but to stop and look, we can hardly unravel it all. It has mutated into some new form that we barely recognize. It may have all started one sunny afternoon when we were five and we fell and hurt ourselves badly, and someone made us stop crying with a threat. After that, any similar situation would only have compounded the effect. When we learn by fear the patterns set very quickly. They can also, however, be tenderly re-set by love. Sometimes this tenderness is evident, and sometimes it comes with painful force, like the re-breaking of a broken bone, that must be re-set in order to heal in the best possible manner. Either way, the energy behind the force is still love.

This love can come from another person, but we are going to find the richest, deepest source in the universe right there under our ribcage…somewhere in the center of us beyond the bones and the tissues. Inside our great hearts the love is waiting, we are just learning to tap into it. Until we can tap into our love, our intuition is likely to be faulty and contaminated by fear, like a river that is polluted too near its source.

Ironically, of course, it is right about the time we begin a relationship with self-love when we meet that special person who can support and reflect us. It is also right about the time our intuition seems to kick in unfailingly and at any time of need. We are just initiating the process by making a place for the stream to flow. We give direction to that stream of support, abundance, and love from the universe when we just put our hands in the dirt a little bit, and dig into what we are afraid of.

When we dig into the fears we find that they only point the way to more of our untapped power and beauty, and when that energy is reclaimed it is as if we suddenly have new friends at our sides. When the tidal waves come we are taught to run, heart pounding, away from them as fast as we can, but whatever stops us in our tracks with panic we should step deeper into...so that we can find the mysterious glory of the revelation on the other side.

When we become fearless we are truly free. The path to fearlessness is of grand proportions, and you are going to need the walking stick of self-love to lean on when you get weary. I couldn't have done justice to you if I had just written a simple book of practices to enhance your intuition. It would be like showing you a beautiful sailboat and giving you no wind to take you across the sea.

The Oracles of ancient times knew this. They knew that intuition is enhanced spontaneously when you remember your own true nature, and therefore the true nature of the universe. Love being the true nature of the universe made the practice of self-love the primary way to embody, honor, and practice that truth. The earliest rituals were performed for the Self, as the most direct connection to the cosmos. Then added to these were rituals honoring the "other" as reflection, for example, nature, animals and deities. Later, the other became separate and god became something thought of as outside of ourselves, rather than our innate essence.

The support which the Oracle sat upon at ancient Delphi in Greece, was called a tripod. It was a seat with three legs. From my memories of the time, in its earliest use, the three legs represented the "three pillars" of self-love, will, and power. These were thought to be the base or foundation for all prophecy or vision. It was understood that self-love was named first because it was by way of self-love that true will and power naturally sprang forth. Therefore, striving for self-love alone was enough to spontaneously create the rest of the support for accessing the other realms of being and wisdom.

Consider self-love to be the first step on the golden path of the Intuitive Life. Yet even before that step the way must be prepared, so let us consider the preparation of the way.

The first thing an Oracle of ancient times was asked to do was a ceremony of self-renewal, before even beginning her or his intuitive life, as well as before each giving of prophecy or remembering. Self-renewal is vastly important to building a relationship with self-love, which is why the Oracles were asked to consider it so deeply when getting themselves ready for the life they would enter into so fully.

To self-renew is to give ourselves permission to start over. Not when we are "complete" with everything under the sun we may have left unfinished, but here and now. Right now.

Self-renewal means forgiving ourselves for whatever may be lingering, and opening our arms to a brand new day, an entirely clean slate, a brilliantly clear canvas waiting for our new self to express. And indeed, that is exactly what it gives us...space.

We often become so confined by the subtle residues of time and the weightier burdens of regret, that we lose sight completely of space. Worse than losing sight we lose the *feeling* that comes from having space. We forget how to breathe and how to move, and how to even speak without thinking and re-thinking until our spontaneity and creativity are reduced to whatever dust is left under the boots of our heaviness inside.

We not only forget the freedom of space, we begin to associate our worth with carrying the burdens. This is reinforced by what we are taught, from early childhood, about self-worth being something you earn, rather than something you already have and continue to nurture with love. We feel that if we let go of the burdens we will be cheating, giving up, shirking responsibility, dropping the ball, or even hurting others somehow.

We fear that if we don't have burdens anymore we will cease to exist, or will be such a rarity that we will have nothing to communicate with others about. We will become an anomaly, a bright spot on a gray sky that others try to erase. Even worse, we fear that we will become a live wire, an electric red flame, an endless rainbow, and that others will see us too well and dislike us for challenging the tiny flame they cup their hands around to hold back the winds of remorse and self-judgment. But we are wrong. How funny that we forget that no matter how others boo and hiss they are aching with the deepest, most desperate hunger to remember and become free. Let them go. Let the ones who would point fingers at you only in order to look away from themselves, go away, shouting insults if they must. Others will come who *want* to see a bright spot in a gray sky. There are legions.

The ones who will do anything to avoid your light are the ones who have become numb, and who would also do anything to avoid feeling again. However, even they will someday feel again, and even they burn beneath the numbness to be free. We all become numb to different degrees. We do it as our last defense against the pain. We do it as our final resort when we feel that the desperation is just too much. The pain is like the fear—it will yield for us the greatest fruits, if we but have the tools to explore it. Numbness is only temporary. We must pass through the gates of the temple of feeling again to be able to transform the fiery pain into liquid life.

So, preparing the way begins not with the expectation that your wounds must all be healed first, that you must have forgiven everyone you have felt hatred toward, or that you must be able to find complete inner peace. That would postpone your joy far too much and so unnecessarily. Preparing the way is as simple as imagining that up until this point in your life you have filled one book completely, and now you are starting another one. This new one could have a new name, new subjects, and is full of pretty new blank pages to be filled with your ecstasy, your longings, and your prayers. In fact this could be a new life completely, and you could be beginning it right now. You don't carry over the table of contents from the last book. You only bring what lights your heart on fire.

When I was nine or ten years old I kept a journal, and if I'd had a hard day, or even if I'd just had negative thoughts about myself or something I did that day in the smallest of ways, I would end my entry with, "and tomorrow I will be a new me."

This was as deeply meaningful to me then as it is now. It meant to me then that a night of sleep could erase anything. It meant that I never had to carry over something from the day before, or from any time before at all that made me feel bad in any way. It was a symbol of the fact that I gave myself permission to start over anytime.

As we "grow up" it is repeatedly pounded into us that we must accrue energies like a bank account accruing interest. We are given so many responsibilities that it feels as if we couldn't possibly leave the day before behind us and start anew. Kids are given so much homework that they hardly have time to relax anymore. Then there is work, which if approached traditionally in our time is like a prison with a very, very long sentence. We get into a lot of these arrangements for security, prestige, or acceptance. The cost is our freedom, and nothing is worth that trade.

It is, however, excellent news, that it is never too late. If you are deeply entrenched it just takes a little more untangling or a really good machete. If you sharpen your blade on the stone of the three pillars, there is nothing you can't cut through, because when you know your true nature you are set free by default. Self-love is what we default to, we just have to disengage all the programs that mix up the essential message and tell us otherwise.

Because let me tell you, the essential message, the one that sings from the trees and the oceans and our souls, is that we are beautiful beyond comprehension. The ultimate message is that we are so radiant that we can burn through any heavy pain or dark constriction. We are endlessly flowing moonbeams of passionately rushing love, and we were given wings to fly through any dimension, any obstacle, across any sky.

We don't need to wait to be empowered. We just need to find a crack in the dam of self-restriction and take a deep breath and blow it wide. Too many great rivers within are held back, and the land of our world is aching for water to rush over it without translation, fixation, or filtration. The world has been in a drought, waiting for the day of perfection to come while we have all the water we need and more, just held back for that final benediction.

We aren't going to love ourselves because we are perfect in the terms we have imagined. We are going to love ourselves because we are more perfect than we could ever hope, because our perfection includes all the little cracks we have been trying to cover up for so long. All the little cracks that only get bigger as we reach to cover them up. They are part of our ever-changing beauty and they have their own wisdom about how to proceed. If we were focusing on our strengths instead of our weaknesses they would, in their own time, begin to disappear.

But again, we won't be waiting for that. If the Oracles of the past had waited for that they would never have fulfilled their destiny, just as we, as the Oracles of today, would never fulfill ours. You see, being an Oracle is not about being the best psychic on your block, it is about having a wider awareness that allows you to see a little more of the background, and the foreground, the future, the present, and the past. It is about a perspective that doesn't come from books, solely from experience, nor from lists of spiritual merit. It comes from getting up really close to yourself in the great cosmic mirror and not shrinking back from your beauty.

That is when you talk to the gods, and if you are really lucky, the goddesses too. That is when you see everything while looking at nothing. That is when you hear the future on the wind and know the answer to any question. You get down on your knees on the dirt floor by the grandest altar of your heart, and keep praying, even when everything draws you outside to distraction. You start by hearing your own heartbeat. Then you can hear the song of the universe, and only then.

There is nothing you have done that is too ugly to forgive. It may need to be deeply acknowledged in order to be rightfully honored and released, but it serves no one for

you to bear it. Free yourself from the binds of old shame,
and though you may feel as if you are escaping wildly into
the night rather than officially crossing the finish line, do
it anyway. There is no finish line. It was all a myth to begin
with. Escape, the kind that feels like nakedness on a warm
night, is the only way to reclaim the most deeply held fears
and unmask them as love.

We will never prove ourselves by accomplishment or
refinement. We won't even prove ourselves by self-love
because there is absolutely nothing to prove. Proof is only
needed as a faulty crutch for crippled faith. We don't need
to prove ourselves to love. We *are* love. To think we have to
prove ourselves in the ever-present light of love is a deeply
impressed delusion that keeps us talking to the walls of
self-confinement. We think it keeps us safe. We think there
might be just too much fresh air in the wild outdoors, but
that wild space is like a womb of glowing light and we could
never feel more warmly held, nor more deeply freed, than
we do among that scented night.

Perhaps self-love feels like a madness from where we stand,
a life lived with an ease that seems foreign, even alien to us.
How funny that it is only a life lived with a light on, always
showing us the way home. It doesn't mean we can't travel
outside its mighty boundaries, only that we know the way back
from our great explorations within. It is just that we have a
little starlight clustering over our special path, illuminating the
way. It simply makes us feel that much more sure-footed and

dissuades our doubts and fears. We feel supported, even during the times of our greatest challenges.

We will find that love, self-love, has been waiting by our door a very long time. It is never too late to let it in. We just have to be willing to believe we can still open. We begin by giving ourselves a chance to start over, and by finding ways to remind ourselves that we have done so when we begin to look back without wanting to. Then we just take it a little easier on ourselves. We just cut ourselves more slack, give ourselves more time, shed undesired expectations, and focus, doggedly, on what makes us feel good about ourselves.

If we all really stand back and get perspective, it doesn't take very long to distinguish which things we do that make us excited and alive, and which drain us. Which people celebrate us, and which criticize us. Which thoughts are pervasively negative about ourselves and inaccurate, exploited, or outdated, and which thoughts are like the buoys that keep us from having to tread the water of insecurity and self-doubt without support. Those thoughts lift us up without taxing our muscles, like the wings of our angels when we have so surrendered that we let them have us, body and soul, to mend. We learn to accept support and say no thank you to negativity, no matter how seductive or deceptive its form. No thank you isn't all that hard to say. It works even in the most sensitive or tricky situations. There are no contracts written that cannot be broken. The universe doesn't work by absolutes. This is where self-love leads us to will, and asks us to take action to support that love…whether by nurturing or the power that rises like the lion toward the sun, ascends like a serpent from the base of your spine, and roars like the ocean from your core. We are afraid that it is rage because it wears the same hat, but that is only the silhouette, they are totally different people underneath. But of course you will only know if you get closer and take a chance.

Insecurity has its place. If we didn't waver between insecurity and security we would cease to be dynamic beings, or to know what security feels like as we change. We just want to allow insecurity to be something we experience and move through, not something we have to live within unnaturally. Still, it is by entering the cave of our insecurities that we are empowered, not by pretending it doesn't exist by burying it in affirmations we don't really feel. The affirmation should be the song that comes from the inside of the cave, whether still in fear or liberated. It should be authentic and a vehicle, rather than a short-cut to a place you haven't even decided you truly want to go.

You are a miracle. You have gifts and treasures beyond even your wildest dreams. You can therefore make miracles in your life blossom as you choose. Intuition is simply the tool to remember that you can. Self-love is the spring from which we drink to become strong enough to prepare to fly, and then it is the wind that carries us anywhere we want to go.

Trust

Holding the Hand of God

"Is there any room for fear in complete trust?"

This is the first question my beings asked me that day. It was my first trip back to Egypt in this lifetime, and I had walked into a temple with no idea that I would be greeted by the beings who would become some of my greatest friends and guides.

I have always known them, and had known many other beings before them in this life as well, but it was not until the moment that they said, "Come in, Sit down…" that I felt so close again to beings of any kind. They welcomed me and we began to talk like old friends from the very beginning. I felt that I could tell or ask them anything. There was nothing too small, too shameful, too mundane. They knew my soul.

The question they asked me that day changed my life. I had always known a fearless part of myself, and recognized its

45

expression when it moved in me, but this question asked me to search even more deeply to find the level at which I could constantly operate in this fearlessness, this trust. It has become an exercise and a perfect reminder of true faith. When I find I am scared I ask myself that question, and the answer is always no and I am relieved of fear.

Is there any room for fear in complete trust?

What is complete trust?

Complete trust is the sense that we are never alone, that there are no mistakes, and that we are always lovingly held by the universe. Complete trust is the knowingness that we exist in an ocean of that love, and that anything that seems contrary to it is an illusion. It may be a powerful illusion, and it may have a purpose and very real-feeling consequences, but it is like watching a play against the backdrop of the sky…if the scene being played becomes too intense you can always refocus on the infinite. It is recognizing that even the pain is like a movie you are watching and that someday it will pass and all that will be left of it is the love.

It isn't that fear doesn't have its place. It's just that we don't want fear driving the boat. We want the winds of the universe…the winds of possibility and promise, to direct us. We want life to be the expression of an open heart. We want to be healthy: body, mind, heart, and soul.

Trust is knowing that however bad things may look at times, there is a deeper reason for them that we may not always see. Sometimes we don't understand that reason for days, or even years. Sometimes we won't understand it until we leave the body and have full awakening again.

Trust is feeling that however we feel we may have done wrong, or been done wrong, the universe and the great love of the divine has not abandoned us, and never will.

Trust is knowing that everything has a perfection, and we are all a part of it. Trust is believing that there is a rightness in all things that will eventually be revealed.

For an Oracle trust was and is paramount, essential. Without trust it was too terrifying to enter into the altered states and depart for other dimensions. The great darkness became like the empty closet at night or the space under the bed for a child. It became a blank canvas to write all one's fears upon. The imagination, rather than an agency of the divine, would become an agency of the fear, coloring all things in a sinister hue.

Trust was and is like the candle that shows us the same things that daylight would on a scary night in the forest...that the trees are still the same trees that shelter us from the bright light of the sun and the cold falling of rain. Trust is like that shelter and comfort that we can take with us anywhere we go. Conditions may get hard, but the trust is a warm blanket that promises softer times to come.

For the Intuitive Life, trust is the life preserver that allows us to move with the undulating bliss of the ocean, without fear of drowning. It allows us to dive as deeply as we want to without fear of being consumed or getting lost. It is something that gives us buoyancy and a lifeline back to the safest shore.

When I was in India my families there took me under their wings like nothing I had ever quite experienced before. I felt like I was nine years old again, or even five, hovering behind my mother while she took care of everything for both of us. Only a few nights after arriving, I experienced one of the longest pujas of the year. It was the Durga Puja and the night's streets were crowded full of people and animals. There were tents erected for Durga as temporary temples every block or so that we walked. Devotional music blared from speakers at each of them, and incense and candles burned and wafted everywhere.

Inside each tent was a clay image of Durga, painted beautifully and ornamented with flowers. Huge colored bulbs lined the streets and sent all the shades of the rainbow into the night. As my friend and dance teacher Chapala led me through the crowds I began to enter a deep trance, all of my senses filled with my surroundings. Looking up at the moon I realized I was beginning to hallucinate, and it occurred to me that I had better stay alert, seeing as it was one of my first nights in India as a woman of just nineteen, alone. But then I remembered I was not alone. Chapala had my hand, and she was holding tight to it as she led us through the throngs and amid the smoky lights and many sounds of the celebration slurring into one another.

I realized that Chapala was not going to let go, and so I could. I realized that if our hands were to separate she would immediately find me and capture my hand again. In other words, I felt safe...in both the most foreign, and yet deeply familiar environment I have ever known.

Knowing trust allows you to feel safe. Knowing that you have a hand to hold onto, that someone or something is looking out for you and caring for you allows you to surrender. Surrendering brings miracles. Having a framework, just as I had Chapala's hand and a sense of her tenacious caring for me, is hugely important. It is like the way that having strong boundaries can allow us to more truly enjoy freedom.

When I was planning my trip to India I was advised of up to twenty various shots and vaccinations I could have, many of them considered essential. I thought about it and decided that I would refuse all of them. I decided that if I were meant to be sick I would get sick, with something there is no vaccination for, or for which the vaccination is only partially effective. I even had the clear feeling that the vaccinations would indeed weaken my immune system, leaving me more vulnerable than protected.

The other very important thing I did, before making my decision against all advice, was to check with myself and see if I felt that the vaccines would serve the purpose of making me "feel" more protected, or helping to convince my mind that I was. I found that there was a place in myself that I had romanticized malaria because of a novel I read many years before, and for that reason, as a precaution, I took with me a medication to prevent malaria. You see, I checked with myself and attempted to discover what trust, what security, what protection felt like to me. It is very individual to each person.

Then, when I was in India I "sensed" my food and scanned it very carefully, checking to make sure I felt right about it before I ate it. Once there was a part of a dish I told my Didi (older sister) that I didn't feel right about. She said it had been brought from the temple rather than home cooked like the rest of what I usually ate. So I had sensed correctly that it might not be right for me, as it may have been made with un-boiled water. It may seem like an extraordinary gift to have such a sense, but I feel so often that we would be surprised at what we "know" when we just check in to see whether something feels right to us or not. So often, it really is that simple. It is when we have a great deal of emotional content with or pressure on a subject that it can be hard to get clear perspective for intuition. The information and practices in this book will address that issue and many more.

Knowing what supports you, what makes you feel comforted and safe, may be truly vital to your feeling of trust. Nesting in that experience will strengthen you, so that those feelings of trust can be transferred into even the most challenging times, making them easier to bear.

One of the greatest poisons to our trust is betrayal, which many of us have experienced so deeply in this world. We may have felt this betrayal from family members, friends, lovers, or even whole groups of people. We may have experienced the feeling of self-betrayal. I know that forgiveness, often paired with time and distance, is a great cure, but forgiveness often has to ripen like a fruit, in its own time. In the meantime, going to the center of your feeling of betrayal and honoring it is an incredible place to begin to unwind its tendrils around your heart.

When I channel the Greek Goddess Hera, she shares her story of healing from betrayal. She says that after being betrayed over and over again she found that it was not her great compassion or discretion which finally took away her pain. She says that it was only when she danced around a fire at night on a mountainside, wailing her agony into the winds that she felt release. Until that time her wounds were still open. She often says that she knows not all of us can or would want to do this, but that telling your story is enough. Just telling your story to someone or something which will truly listen, whether it is a good friend, a pen and paper, an intuitive or counselor, your animal companion, or the ocean. Telling your story lets the poison out.

If, when we get to the center of our sense of betrayal, we find that we feel betrayed by god, by the universe, by life, then that is the first betrayal to address. Start by telling that story, because as you explain why you feel betrayed by life, you will hear new things coming out of its telling that heal the core of a great wound. You may have to tell it many times, or just a few, but when you reconnect with your sense of trust in life, everything will change.

Trust comes a lot easier when we decide we have nothing to lose. When we empty the hoards in our cupboards and lighten the loads we carry. I always remember this when I think about losing my life. Sometimes, when I used to fly alone and the plane would hit serious turbulence, I would become afraid for a few moments that my life was in danger. But then I'd remember that if I completely trust the universe, I would know that I could only die when the time was right. Not just right but perfect, since there are no mistakes. And then I would relax, and no matter how much the plane bumped along I would feel safe. I told myself, "I am a delicate flower in the protective hands of god."

When you forget what support feels like you can always simply find a piece of earth and lie down on it. Just close your eyes and breathe, or leave them open and relax them on the stars, the clouds, or the brilliant blue sky. Merely to meditate on the feeling of the earth holding your body like a warm hand can bring forward powerfully the sensation of being supported.

Sometimes we just haven't been touched in a long time... touched in a true and deep way. Sometimes we really just need to be held by loving arms, caressed on the cheek, told with a soft voice that everything is going to be okay. When there is not someone in our lives that can give us that physical reassurance and love, we must have great patience and faith, sometimes at a level that seems impossible. Those are the times we must draw even more from nature, other forms of companionship, creativity, and our guides.

This is what we trusted in the temples…the warm stone beneath our feet, the sunsets and moonrises, the ability of the heart to open against all odds, the way that laughter eventually finds you no matter where you hide, the blooming of flowers into the sun, the feeling of hot tears, the moans of the body, the running of water, the cresting of bliss over everything. We went bare-footed and bare-hearted, transmuting the excess inclination toward self-protection into pure faith.

When you have your support, the place you know you can put your faith, it allows you to feel that you can travel freely into the lands of intuition. The Oracles at Delphi had their secure three-legged chair. It is said that it was designed to hold the Priestess in place so that she would not fall into the chasm at the height of her ecstatic frenzy, but that was not the only reason. The true reason was derived from its symbolism and actuality as the support to create a grounded, nurturing place for the Pythia to travel from, and bring through the oracular guidance.

When we are held we grow wings. We often think that when we can stand alone we achieve peace, freedom, alignment with the divine. In one sense it is true, but in a holistic sense it is inorganic, in that we are all part of a oneness. I always say we are *meant* to have help. It is part of the design of our creation and of the universe that we flourish most by inter-action and the dynamic exchange of loving, supportive energy.

Humans can't always uplift us, though sometimes we are indeed very, very lucky to have uplifting friends and loved ones in our lives. However the universe is a never-ending wellspring of support and love. And beings, well, beings just absolutely live for the moments they can inspire and uplift. Their hearts light up with absolute joy when they can be of any help or service.

Again, we are *meant* to have help. This same support can come from nature, inspiration, friendships, creativity, or many other places of reflection. Only you can decide what feels supportive to you, and stay aware of it as it may change. Sometimes the Oracles would rely on ritual that had been handed down to them and that they trusted to support them on their journeys, sometimes on the energies of nature and the earth, and sometimes on beings, goddesses, or gods which they aligned with.

Somewhere inside we remember the times in which it felt like the answers were so much closer to the questions. It was as if every move and every expression were made with the absolute blessing of the goddess or god and the rightness of it all reso-nated back to you in each moment. It is possible to live that way here and now in this world.

If there isn't any fear in complete trust, then all of the ener-gy spent holding back, second guessing, and being full of doubt is freed up to be invested in your creativity, your joy, and your true wealth, and suddenly living the Intuitive Life becomes the natural result of restored and abundant energy.

Like the plants in the garden that just need something to lean on in order to thrive, when we are supported, we naturally blossom.

THE ORACLE WITHIN

Imagination

The Forgotten Secret

When we are at our very youngest our imaginations are often nourished. We are encouraged by the books and games that we are exposed to. We are told about Santa, the Easter Bunny, and the Tooth Fairy. We are encouraged to draw, to sing, to make up stories. Most of our world may have been created from the land of make-believe, from playing house to pretending to be wild animals. Even with toys whole scenarios were made up so they could interact. They were named and given personalities. You could fly. You could live in a palace, or a desert, or go to the moon. In the imaginary land you could do anything.

You know what I am about to say. Your stomach may be turning a little bit as you think about it, because what happened next was a kind of death for most of us. Everything took a turn at some point and it was time to understand "reality." Because according to most people in our culture, there is a certain time for make-believe and then you have got to "get real" or you will "never make it in the world."

Everything changes at school. Storytime becomes history and make-believe becomes the memorization of facts. With imagination it can be any way you like, with facts you are either right or wrong, and there is no in-between. You go from being described to being graded, from an individual to a letter and series of numbers. The hugeness of "you" is reduced to something small, your infinity to something finite, graspable, labelable, and categorizable.

It becomes about how you perform rather than how much fun you are having. It becomes about standardization rather than uniqueness...how you compare to others. It becomes about "fitting in" and blending in, rather than about standing out, and indulging in what makes you special and different.

It is made clear that make-believe and the realm of imagination are not real. In many cases it is pounded into us until we believe that someone who dreams or plays is to be laughed at, or certainly at least not taken seriously. Those with a strong imagination are suddenly called "day-dreamers" and marked down for it. Or they are called unrealistic, idealistic, naïve, immature, inexperienced. All of this for remaining innocent in a world that has accepted certain rules and learned to play the game.

Some of us only buy into the game in a few areas of our lives. Areas where we have the most fear, or that we were most persuaded to excel, get serious, or become super-responsible.

In that way the imagination becomes disenfranchised and we forget about another responsibility, the one we have to our soul to never forget how to play and dream. At some point each of us realizes that heaviness is a dead-end street, and when the gravity really begins to take its toll, we start to understand that we must find a reversal.

We often approach accessing intuition with this serious-ness, and while it is indeed a seriously profound and important pursuit, it is with a light and playful heart that we will find the most supreme realizations and understanding.

One of the greatest secrets is that imagination, left in the box with our childhood toys, is the key to receiving visions and information intuitively. It is the key to unlocking the doors to the other worlds, and without it we may be able to pick some locks, but we won't have nearly the success and ease we would have with it always in our pockets.

You see, imagination *is* the vehicle we use to receive intui-tive information. It is the same channel that this information comes through…the one you used to play house or race cars when you were little. It is rather like the two uses of the esoph-agus, one for breathing and the other for eating and drink-ing. It simply has both capacities. Imagination can be both something we use to run silly meaningless things through our minds, and it can be our greatest vessel for intuitive connection and creative power.

In the intuition trainings that I offer, I can't tell you how common a theme it is that someone is held back from intuitive expansion because as soon as it begins to come through they believe it is "just their imagination." I understand this intimately because of the way that I struggled as a little girl, being taught that make-believe was one thing, but calling it real was a lie. I didn't want to lie, and I felt deeply right in my heart about what was happening to me, but I knew it happened in the imaginal realm, and it was incredibly hard for me to make peace with that. I kept asking myself if I was being dishonest. It was like a paradox, that something could be both imaginary and real. And yet isn't that what we call magic? Isn't that where the mysteries of the universe make miracles happen? Isn't that where everything begins and ends?

What kept me going through those years was the deeper knowingness that whatever I had been taught in this life, there was even more within me to take into consideration. For instance, I knew I had experienced other civilizations and times in which these gifts were fostered, and not only believed to be real, but indeed more real than the outside world. I knew that somewhere, someone else must know that it was from the inner world that the outer world was born.

Still, this conditioning about imagination runs deep. And in its essence, it is deeply beautiful that we are so committed to authenticity that we don't wish to spread falsity into the world, or to falsify ourselves. That is why it is so important to know how to walk the fine line that allows us to truly interpret what comes to us intuitively.

First however, it is essential to enhance our imaginations once again. We can do this by reading a well-written and beautifully described story, or simply by taking a walk and imagining, with detail, what it would feel and look like to have our dreams come true. We could just dream again in general. It is like opening the flow to something we may have shut off the valve for a long time ago, or instead of accepting a trickle, allowing a spring or a river to nourish our imaginative capacities.

We can also do this by actually forcing an imaginary vision. Maybe we can't see the temple, or the goddess or the person's aura spontaneously. As long as we allow ourselves to simply experiment, without involving anyone else until it is time, we can simply *imagine* these things and then sort through what we experienced for the parts that may feel authentic or important. That is just another way to open the flow which then becomes automatic when tuning in.

A lot of people tell me that they can feel things intuitively, or sometimes even hear messages, but that they just can't get visuals and they wish that they could. When those same people are asked to *imagine* that they see something they are looking for, unless they have something else holding them back, they always have the vision. We are often afraid that we will only see what we want to see, again wanting authentic input. That is understandable, but we have to start somewhere to open up to the inner worlds, and if we need to begin by seeing what we want to see, then so be it.

Once we are more clear on at least being able to imagine what we are looking for and strengthening the muscle of that capacity, then we can move on into discerning and interpreting. Then we can begin to become an artist of the intuitive realms. Two intuitives could get the very same vision or information and interpret it in quite different ways. That is why, whether we are learning to receive information only for ourselves or for others, we want to be as clear a vessel as we can be, using as few personal filters as possible. The next chapter on surrender will address this further.

We often have to deal with "guardians at the gate" of our intuitive world. There are a few different kinds. Some, like the Sphinx forever guarding the records, are there to initiate you and reflect you to yourself. Others are simply dark illusions that ask us to check our fears before entering. They repeat to us all the negative things we have been told about intuition, and encourage us to share the mass-consciousness or worldview about it. They sometimes want to undermine our very sense that intuition is valid. The good news is that they are flimsy and made of paper, and their arguments are old and already cracking under the weight of a deeper truth. We just have to be brave enough to walk by them. Because the reality is that they can't truly put up a fight. They simply aren't substantial enough, and will certainly blow away like dry leaves at the sight of the power of your deeper knowing.

The term or word 'discernment' sounds so clear and so cut-and-dry. The first thing we should know about the intuitive world is that it is not made of bricks and fractions. It is a watery-seeming world, interconnected and vast. It is important to know that even discernment has a different context in these realms.

To give an example, I often write down what my beings share with me when I go to them. They rarely, if ever, appear when I am working with others, since it is the person's own guides who usually come, so it is when I myself am in need of guidance that I go to them. Desire is so important in the accessing of intuition—the true heart's desire to know, or to see, or to understand. For when we understand we are relieved of burden, and shown the freedom to do something different that we hadn't known we could before.

As I listen to my beings I am hearing them in my head, if you will, rather than the way I hear someone talking to me across a coffee table "out loud." I can see them in front of me, and as they talk to me I have noticed a specific sort of pattern that sometimes emerges. At certain points when they are speaking, it sounds like the voice of my own mind or heart. It sounds just like I do when I talk to myself and give myself good advice. Or it sounds exactly like the things I have already been telling myself about that particular topic. It is so familiar that I feel like I am talking to myself. Then, in another part of the same sentence or series of phrases, it is suddenly much more clearly coming from "outside" of me and they are saying things I would never think to say, or hadn't known at all. All this can happen many times back and forth as I listen to what my beings have to share.

There are a couple of reasons why it can seem so familiar to receive guidance, whether it is through connection to your guides, or straight from the universe in the form of a message, sign, or vision. One is that the universe and your guides know you very, very well. In fact, the reason certain beings are your guides is because you are very close and have a lot in common. And, much like two good friends or lovers who can finish each other's sentences, you and your beings are on the same track in many ways. The other reason that you may have already been telling yourself the things you hear when you tune into your intuition is because life, the universe, and your guides have often been trying to get the message across for some time!

Even deeper than that though, is the recognition that you actually know all the answers already anyway. In that place where we contain everything, we also know everything, and in using our intuition or connecting with beings we are simply seeking confirmation.

Confirmation is hugely important, and it doesn't mean we don't trust ourselves enough or that we are overly insecure. It can be merely a way to get a reflection, a reassurance. Once again, it has to do with the support that allows us to take flight. Sometimes we just need to hear it from someone else, too… especially when it holds a lot of importance for us. It is like getting a second opinion from another doctor, or being able to check a special mirror for your blind spots.

Once in a while it is nice to not always have to be vigilantly planted in the driver's seat, but to let someone else that you trust drive, so that you can fall asleep in the back of the car on the way home.

We do not have to accept everything we get intuitively. We can take our time to feel it out, especially if we are just getting used to the other worlds. We are not signing contracts or taking vows because we decide to go deeper into our intuition. We are remembering to play, attempting to trust, and allowing our imagination to be the craft we use to glide through the great waters.

Intuition is not the dark, ominous world of fate and foreboding. It is not a book that is written and finished. It is a journey that reveals to you the amazing possibilities you may have forgotten. It gets you out of tight corners, clothing that doesn't fit you, and the prisons we can all feel trapped in at times. It is an eye-opener and a way-maker. It is a chance to believe again, and to find resources you didn't know that you had.

Imagination is the back door that leads into the privacy of the woods and the flower gardens behind your house. It holds magic and chance and hope. It is the place where the dreams begin and are set into motion to become part of your physical world, and it is the vehicle you can use to travel the dimensions, and to view your life from a whole new perspective.

Just imagine.

Surrender

Altered States, Trance, Ecstasy

There is a reason why at one period of time the Oracle of Delphi only gave prophecy under the effects of the ethylene that rose from the earth in the sacred sanctum of the temple. There is a reason that people around the world have used sound, chant, toning, or mantra to affect altered states. There is a reason that tribes of native peoples stretching from one farthest reach of our Earth to the other have engaged in ritual dances that elicited states of trance, or practiced a sacred sexuality that honored the creative and ecstatic properties of union and pleasure.

It is because these altered states, whether trancelike or ecstatic, produce a kind of surrender that nourishes the soul, and opens us up to worlds beyond our own. From these worlds we can gain wisdom that may afford us greater understanding of our true nature, or lend us knowledge about how to heal.

When we can surrender, we are acknowledging spontaneously that there is something we can surrender to. That there is a great force that will hold us, even when we let go of everything. We are acknowledging that we don't have to keep everything in the universe or even in our own lives together, that it is both entirely within and entirely out of our hands. We are giving up our problem-solving abilities and our burdens, and we are giving in to a flow that captures our soul in rhythm and bliss. We are leaving the realm of the quantifiable and entering the realm of the unknown and the indefinable.

It is often a sobering world we live in, and we are taught to be sober about it. We are supposed to go to work in a sober mind-frame and socialize in one. We wonder why so many people are absorbed into addictions…to escape from the mind-numbing reality of this sobriety about life. Abuse of certain behaviors or substances has replaced the rightful space for surrender in our lives. When we have a healthy dose of surrender, trance, altered states, or ecstasy in our lives, we don't need to escape. We don't need to escape in that case because we are free to explore…there is nothing to escape from.

Countless ancient rituals were dedicated to surrender and to exploring the balance between what is thought of as waking reality, and what lies in the realm of liberation, fantasy and freedom. We shrink back from fantasy, afraid we will get lost and live our whole lives in one, but in doing so we forget the powerful balance that allowing ourselves this surrender can bring. Much like we can reach the intuitive realms through imagination, we can reach the realm of creative genius through the liberation that is brought on by release and the realm of the fantastic.

In our modern day, since many of us don't get the chance to practice the ancient rituals of trance, ecstasy, and altered states, we find them in either the more current or the timeless versions. Some of us get lost in dance and movement, or use sound much as it was used before, as a tool to enter trance or ecstasy. Some of us find this release in an intense hike, or traveling to an entirely new and different place. Some of us find it in meditation. Some of us don't find it until something drastic happens in our lives and we are forced to surrender whatever we have been holding tightly to.

Some of us find it in laughter or in a very deep cry. Some of us find it with that one extra drink of wine that just loosens us up a bit. Some of us find it when we get deep bodywork that frees up the tight places inside of us.

Some of us avoid surrender. All of us may do it sometimes. We do it because we don't know what will happen if we surrender, and we are afraid. As if, like becoming too drunk at a dinner party, we will say all the wrong things, or worse yet, expose ourselves to something we would not have wanted to if clear-minded.

We do not want to deeply surrender and enter an altered state at just any time. Sometimes we really need to know that we can be lucid. There are situations in which it is of great importance. You see, this is not about holding surrender, altered states, or trance in higher esteem than clarity and lucidity. It is simply about making a place for both, and understanding how to find the release that is required to enter into the intuitive realms with most ease and depth.

For example, if we sit down after getting home from a big day, having been in many varied situations already and try to instantly tune in to guidance, we are more likely to get some interference. That interference is an accumulation of all the things your body, mind, and heart have been feeling or thinking that day that didn't get explored. So if you had a breakfast that didn't quite feel right but you had to rush off to an appointment, you didn't really get to address the feeling. Or maybe someone was rude to you but you were in public and needed to stay calm in that environment. All those things will rise up to the surface as soon as you sit down to tune in. And they are in the front of the line.

Until you do something to acknowledge, address, and release these feelings and thoughts, they will be active in your consciousness and slow or cloud the intuition that you may be trying to access. The good news is that we don't have to be able to perform all-night ceremonies or reach the infinite bliss in order to do this. It can take just a few minutes to allow some access to release. Although the deeper the surrender goes, the deeper the revelations may be, to get intuitive information on a daily basis one would not always have to go that deep. I will address many ways of approaching this.

You see, when I was a little girl and would "pass out" and come back with information, I believe this was a remnant of past experience and training as an Oracle. My ideas of what I did or didn't know as a child were not allowing some of the information to come in consciously. Therefore it was only by this act of passing out that I was able to surrender to a different level of consciousness. I was becoming unconscious, and by leaving my conscious mind behind I could discover and receive information beyond that which had been in my conscious awareness before.

The night my Mother asked me if I could pass out on purpose was a turning point, and a great success. For I found that not only was the process just as successful when I "made myself" pass out, it was actually more successful because I was bringing my conscious self with me. It was in the act of pretending to pass out…the act of letting go entirely of my body and falling back onto the bed, that I gave myself permission to let go. It was symbolic of surrendering myself to the process.

When the Oracle of Delphi took in the sacred *pneume*, or gases, it allowed her to surrender her usual thoughts, judgments, and limitations, and simply give herself to the experience. However we mustn't lose sight of her foundation. For

surrendering yourself to something without foundation can
be destructive to the soul. Just as the Pythia rested on the
three-legged chair or tripod while going into the altered states
produced by the ethylene, so as not to follow those who, early
in the discovery of the gases, threw themselves into the vapor-
ous chasm in ecstatic frenzy, and died.

We too are not looking to throw ourselves into the
chasm. Although it is also not about fear, and we can always
start over, we are looking to receive the blessings of the ecstatic or altered states without the consequences of losing what
we have no foundation for. If you remember, the symbolism
of the foundation the Pythia sat upon was the three pillars of
self-love, will, and power. We will talk more about these later,
but when we speak of will and power we are talking about
their true, pure and natural form which your soul exudes.
When these three things are in place, one can surrender freely.

This can also mean choosing the right energetic environment or company—setting the right space, another form of
foundation, for letting go. Once again, when we are supported, we can surrender freely.

That's why the kind of surrender you feel when you get
too drunk and do something you later regret, or the kind of
surrender you might have given to an abusive relationship,
is different than the spiritual surrender we speak of now.
In those cases your foundation of self-love, will, and power
was not in place to support you. When you have this strong

foundation, and make your space and company reflect it, you can safely and joyfully experience the ecstatic release and altered states that create great liberation, revelation, and a new or expanded perspective.

There is a perfect flow in the universe, and a unique one for each of us. We can always tell, whether we acknowledge it or not, when we are out of sync with this natural rhythm. This natural rhythm has all the answers and knows the way in and out of any situation that could arise. It knows how to express our deepest self in the world through our creativity and relationships, and it knows how to keep us in perfect health—whatever that may mean to each of us. The trouble is, we often end up imposing other rhythms over that deepest essence and forgetting all about it. It becomes something that bleeds through in the few surrendered moments we find ourselves in…when we do something we love and allow ourselves to get lost in it. Then we sense the rhythm coming back, and we remember.

The rhythms we impose often begin early. If we were lucky we had the chance to explore or embody our natural rhythms when we were very young, if we had strict parents, however, it may have been imposed upon a great deal even then. Certainly once we start school, unless we had a very unique school experience, those natural rhythms are impressed upon greatly. Our time is metered, our intelligence often stifled, and our creativity graded. Next we are often restrained by a job or worries of money. We frequently override our natural rhythm because we are taught that it is literally what life is about…giving up whatever we really love to just get by. We get used to compromising in whatever ways we have to in order to "make a living," or care for our family or ourselves, or to be liked and attain a "success" that may never fulfill us. We end up extending this compromise into every aspect of our lives, into our relationships and our dreams, until there is very little left to believe in and that deepest rhythm has been quieted.

Of course that deepest rhythm can't go very far. It can be repressed only so long, because it is stronger than anything that could hold it back. We may hold it back for a decade, a few decades, or even a lifetime, but it is going to catch up with us in the next one if we do. It lives on beyond any hindrance to its glory. What is inside you that moves you, can never die.

There are also the less extreme cases…sometimes we are "almost" living at one with that deepest rhythm, but are still making compromises that we think we have to, that we may have been trained to in order to feel self-worth, or out of subconscious feelings of obligation. Those feelings of obligation and compromise have run deep in the rivers and weaves of the mass consciousness for a long, long time now, and it is natural for us to feel impacted by that until we consciously disengage ourselves from them.

When I was in Egypt recently, I had my second chance to experience the profound temple of Abydos. Standing in one of its inner sanctums, I began to hear my heart beat all of a sudden. I felt the presence of Isis, and then heard her telling me that she was adjusting the rhythm of my heart. It was sublime and surreal to actually listen to my heartbeat begin to slow and change as she worked with me. She told me that I had been speeding it up too much, trying to do too many things at once for too long. She was adjusting it back to its "natural rhythm," which would help to slow the pace of my life again. Luckily we don't need to go to Egypt, nor have Isis whisper in our ears, in order to get back to our natural rhythms. We just have to surrender. In fact, Isis is whispering in your ear right now, and we are simply taking the steps to allow you to hear what she is telling you, as a message from your own heart.

Perhaps our own natural rhythm is slower than the one we are functioning with, perhaps it is faster, perhaps there is just a more or less dynamic range than the one we are living with now. Surrender will help lead us to discover and live by this rhythm. To surrender is to know that the train may never stop at the town we were waiting for, and if it is taking us farther from home, we have just got to jump. There is no perfect moment to join in the music…you haven't missed your cue nor should you feel you have to wait for it. You will not find the perfect note to enter on, unless it finds you, and it can only find you if you give in. Surrendering is about discovering what is under the layers of planning, inhibition, and imposed behavior. Who would you have been if no one had ever criticized you? Who you are.

It's never too late.

How do you jump off the train without breaking any bones? Just know that the train isn't even real, and that the whole landscape will change when you get lost in the moment. Because again, when we are already anchored in the divine we can get lost over and over again and never lose anything. That is the real way not to break any bones when we make our leap…by recognizing that we have nothing to lose, even if it seems like we do. We have to let go of what we think we need to hold onto, or at least get back to asking ourselves the question: Why am I holding onto this?

Altered states happen when we let go of the state of mind we regularly inhabit. We have entire worlds of perception available to us, and in this life, and in this time, we are taught to pick one and put on blinders to the others. We then become afraid of the others, for the same reason we become afraid of the dark, because we can no longer see what is in them. When we allow ourselves, safely and with our foundation in place, to enter altered states, we are taking the blinders off and finally seeing again all the rest that the universe and our higher selves have to offer. All those other worlds open up again and we are not afraid anymore. The worst fears we face are not so much in those other worlds as they are in the moment of removing the blinders, and all we imagine might happen to us if we let go.

We fear we will dissolve and our identity will be swallowed up by the greater primal forces of the universe. In truth, they are our own greater primal forces, and they represent more of us, the parts of us we have been taught to repress or are afraid to express. We imagine that as our identity falls we will be naked, overly revealed. We fear that we are risking everything and will be laughed at, ostracized, and lose our friends, our jobs, even the way we know ourselves.

Sounds great to me. Losing old ideas of the self. Losing a job that isn't really our work, (if we are afraid of losing it, then it usually isn't really our work). Losing the friends who wouldn't understand who you truly are, and being laughed at. If we can't be laughed at and learn to keep dancing anyway, then we will never be stronger than the opinions of others, and that is a fate I would not wish anyone. To be able to let the world fall down around you if it must, and to keep dancing if there is still a song in your heart. That is what I would wish anyone who still believes there is something more than whatever holds them back.

Altered states are tricky for many, because they sometimes take us right to our fears first, so that we can move through them into the other worlds...like the anxiety that arises before anything else when we are taking the blinders off. We just have to be able to call the bluff, if you will. That is why we want the three pillars strongly beneath us, because they show us the illusion of our fears and support us through to the revelations and bliss waiting on the other side.

Ultimately that is what we will find. Bliss. Whether we wait to die in order to surrender, or whether we surrender to it on a daily basis, it is ecstasy that waits beyond all else. When we enter altered states we have a tool to use for surrender, and if we have our foundation in place we can move through the fears quickly and find ourselves among the bounty of our true nature. That's what it is all about. Altered states are gateways for surrendering to that reality.

Trance is a sustained altered state, often brought on by rhythmic or repetitive stimulus. A wonderful example would be the trance brought on by music, especially rhythmic music or music which contains repeated phrases, like mantras. These sounds set off a series of physical responses in the body having to do with relaxation and release, which have their parallels in the release of the spirit and soul. We are not disembodying the spirit and soul, we are simply giving them space to dance, to redefine, and to take new expression. In fact, we are making even more opportunities for them to embody, to become one with the body.

We can attain trance by dancing, or with any movement, again often repetitive or interpretive in nature. At this level we engage the body literally and give it a chance to find freedom. The more often we dip into this pool of ecstasy and release, the deeper our connection to ultimate creativity and awareness becomes. It doesn't matter if we are dancing in front of our mirror alone at home, or in a room full of other people. What matters is that we get lost in it.

We can enter trance doing handiwork or looking out at the ocean. We can enter trance watching a candle flame or observing at a pattern on the wall. That which hypnotizes has the potential to bring on trance, and the state of trance offers us the potential to transcend. Once we let ourselves, it becomes surprisingly easy to enter trance.

We can find it through becoming aware of our breath, spinning wool, painting, or looking at the moon. It's what we do with, and in our state of trance that matters. If we remain unaware then it is just tuning out, or "spacing out" as we call it. Spacing out, and the world's epidemic with tv, are just a couple of examples of how our culture makes up for missing the experiences of trance that are intrinsic to being alive. It can't be erased, and the substitutes are numbing. They will do when we are desperate to get out of our daily reality, but they often do not feed the soul.

I am not saying that tv or movies are a bad thing, it is how we use them that matters. Sometimes they are a way to lift out of our current perspective and see things from someone else's eyes. Sometimes they are a way to view another world or to fantasize again. Once again, it is how we engage or don't engage, and what we engage with that makes the difference.

We can find altered states by surrendering to our creativity as well. Whether we are devoting ourselves to a creative project or just allowing our imagination to flourish, we can remember how to play. Just to play, whether anything is "produced" from it or not. When we were little we didn't build sand castles to live in.

Another way to enter altered states and discover ecstasy
is through sexual and sensual pleasure. Though they are often
related, they can be two quite different things as well. Sensual
pleasure involves the senses. It is the pleasure brought on by
a delicious meal, the smell of a rose, the feeling of silk or the
wind on your skin, the sound of a beautiful voice, the radiance
of looking at nature or the face of a loved one. Our world is
endlessly filled with these sensual pleasures. They are all around
us all the time.

We learn to tune out these sensual pleasures in order to be
productive and functional. We learn not to stop and smell the
roses. We learn not to fall in love too much, and to phase out
the music in the background, the song of birds, even the taste
of what we are eating sometimes. Or we learn to live without
sensual pleasures. We tell ourselves we can't afford good food, the
best fabrics, our favorite music. We say we don't have time for a
long walk, a scented bath, a barefoot walk in the grass. We get so
used to living without these things that we begin to avoid them
on purpose so we won't experience the sadness of the true realization that we have lived without them for so long.

Yes, there are some pleasures that take time or money, and
there are millions that are free and quick. It is how we indulge
in them that makes them rich and nourishing or not. It is
letting ourselves feel again. And even more, we will discover
that as we start to truly indulge in the sensual pleasures that
are "free and quick" and all around us all the time, we will
ironically somehow find our lives opening in ways that give us

more time and money. We have to say yes to ourselves first, and make a practice of it. Especially when we have made a practice of saying no for a long time.

Sensuality and sensual pleasure are a gateway to self-love, which naturally has the potential to extend into sexuality, whether with oneself or another. Sexuality, for all its reputation, is very simple at its heart. It is just one more potential for expression of love and the experience of the ecstasy we are all made of. If sex has become something different than that for you, you can always go back to exploring self-love and sensual pleasure, because as you deepen into those more joyous experiences, authentic sexual expression is likely to be a natural extension. Again, if you are not in relationship to another sexually, (or even if you are) this expression of your sexuality and generation of pleasure, and even ecstasy can be experienced with yourself.

That may mean putting on your favorite outfit, taking in a play or movie that excites you, or actual physical self-pleasuring. It is time, if it wasn't long, long ago, that being intimate with ourselves becomes a matter of spiritual discussion again, and that self-pleasuring becomes a part of that discussion as well. It doesn't have to be for everyone, but it is certainly a natural and healthy expression of the life experience. We were not born with nerve endings to have to wait for the perfect other person to arrive, nor to have to ignore them.

Life is happening all around us, and it does not exclude you or anything within you or me. When we surrender, the "shadow" self is integrated naturally, and we become stronger than our fears. When we experience pleasure, in whatever way it arrives, the natural response is to surrender...because it feels good. We don't feel afraid because we feel good. We then easily realize that we could open to other worlds of perception that may feel good as well. We sense the ultimate goodness in the universe, and that it is with us at all times. We become free, more and more in our lives. Then intuition simply becomes a way of life, the way we live, not something we have to strive for.

The gases that the Oracle at Delphi inhaled are purported to have been ethylene. Ethylene stimulates the pleasure center of the brain. It is also said that within nature it acts to help plants know when to fruit, blossom, and shed, just as pleasure can remind us of our own natural timing to express and to let go. It is from this state that the Oracle would reach the other worlds, channel the goddesses and gods, and offer guidance. It was through pleasure, altered states, and trance that she found surrender, and through surrender, that she found god.

Nature

The Ultimate Reminder

I remember a lifetime when I lived by the ocean, and unlike times that I knew or worked with others who remembered, in this lifetime I was the only one. At least, at first I was the only one. It isn't that there weren't kind people around me, it is just that even they had forgotten so many things about our origins, our purpose, and the inspiration for living.

In that lifetime in the area where I lived there were no schools, no temples established, no spiritual community to speak of. There were stories, fragmented myths, and half-hearted shrines erected to deities that no one could remember why they were worshipping. So the fact that I was born remembering was not supported or contextualized. I was not noted at a young age for those qualities and chosen for any order of initiates or priestesses, however I was not shunned either. People found my nature unique and interesting, and humored the odd-seeming aspects of my personality. They did so because they felt something warm around me that they could not explain, and they knew it to be good. However mostly, I was left alone.

This is how I discovered the ocean. Not the way in which we discover the ocean as the body of water you reach after a bar of sand or rocky cliff...but the true discovery of the ocean. This is how I learned the language of nature, and it taught me everything.

We can find teachers in this life in so many forms, and nature is one of the most pure and potent of them all, if we can simply learn to hear it speaking to us. In the lifetime I am speaking of I had the gift of listening, and the gift of time. I spent hours and hours leaning over rocky ledges and just watching, and listening to the sea. At first I didn't hear any-thing out of the ordinary, nor did I see anything unusual...only by committed visits for hours at a time did the other, unspoken dimensions of her amazing mystery begin to open themselves to me.

You see, I had no one to talk to about what I knew, that seemingly no one else around me had any idea of, no matter their age, background, or experience. Since no one understood me, I began to tell the ocean and the trees. They were always there, and at first I spoke to them just to be able to say the things there was no space for anywhere else. Then, over time, I spoke to them to hear what they had to say in response. No, they didn't use words like the others. They spoke in waves of energy that you had to become so familiar with, that you could translate them into understanding. No matter how unnatural the issues I shared with them seemed, they understood and had a natural response to them...one that brought all of reality into the realm of the natural. They knew all, like we do when we remember. You see, they just never forget, and never forgot. When we all entered into the Great Forgetting, they held onto the memory for us so we would always have a place to go when we were ready, or needed, to remember.

When humans attempt to destroy the earth or natural world, it is symbolic of, and an extension of the Great Forgetting. It is the last effort to forget...to remove anything around us that will remind us of who we truly are and what we truly come from: love, perfection, and beauty. Just as the earth is stronger than those attempts, the memory will always be stronger than the forgetting. The memory is ultimate, the forgetting is temporary.

It was the Ocean in that lifetime that reminded me why I had come, and what the others had forgotten. And more than anything she confirmed for me, reflected to me, what I already knew but had not had affirmed in any other way in that life. Affirmation is an incredible gift, and one that we are meant to have like a reassuring touch from the universe to show us we are on the right path. Many times it is not just an insecure need, but the celebration of the joy of reflection and remembering.

When I noticed others around me in trouble or suffering, I would share the message from the ocean which could offer them relief or healing. In having a source of direct revelation or divine inspiration, the people of my land at that time became filled with renewed hope. They began to visit me daily with offerings, much as it was at the temples of so many times and places, and ask me questions. I created a special place in the woods by the sea where I had always felt its power most profoundly, and where the people could come to consult with me.

At first only I could hear the voice of the ocean responding to their questions, and I would translate the words and give them the message, but over time there were others who wanted to learn, and I began to teach them even more of what I knew. Soon, they began to be able to hear nature speak to them as well. Sometimes they doubted, but I helped remind them of the ultimate truth that lived inside of them, and the doubts would eventually be dispelled from their hearts forever. They remembered too.

When you learn things there may always be doubts, but when you actually experience or remember them, their truth is self-evident and unshakable.

Over time the people built a temple by the ocean, and it existed long after as a place where people could go to hear the messages from the sea through an intermediary like myself, or where they could go to learn themselves the ancient art of hearing God in everything. This is how these sacred places and sacred arts began, before books were written or mystery schools were founded, there were people who felt different and listened closely, for many hours, to the sea, or to the wind, or to the sound of their own voices.

The natural world can remind us of our own true nature certainly, but it can also give us signs and point us toward the extension of that true essence into our future. The Oracles of Dodona in Greece would listen to the sounds of the wind through the sacred Oak trees and hear prophecies within them. Like my story, it began as a special place within an Oak grove where the priestesses and priests would walk with bare feet and sleep on the ground. Only later would it become temple, school, and cultural center.

It was the same in my earliest memories at Delphi. The cult of Apollo had not yet entered the scene, and it was the earth mother goddess Gaia or Ge that we worshipped and spoke for then. The place we spoke from was the spring, before any temple was built. We could hear the great mother speaking to us through the waters that bubbled up from within her. We could see visions in the reflections of those waters. That is what we spoke of when the pilgrims came then.

The myth says that Apollo came and slew the "python" in the great fissure of the earth, for henceforth he became the being who gave prophecy in that place. It was an allusion to replacing the goddess worship, represented by the python or serpent. However it would always be women who gave the oracles at Delphi, though elsewhere in the world both men and women have been Oracles, and they would always be called

"Pythia" after their beloved Goddess, as a remnant of that sacred past. Apollo was not a bad god or evil being, he is just another representation of the divine who was brought in by those humans who thought him to be the "real" or right one.

In Egypt it began and ended for us with that rich black soil and the waters of the Nile. We could never forget life itself, its origins and nature when this life-giving river flowed through our desert and provided us with everything we needed. The nile was fertility, the nile was life for us. We knew our own great souls were in attendance, we knew Isis and Osiris were still with us when we looked into the sky and saw Orion and Sirius, and when every year the river flooded and washed the banks with that most nourished soil. We knew we were not forsaken, and that we must not be alone.

Egypt was different. It was the birthplace of humanity and of the earth, so we had placed signs everywhere from the earliest times, many of which remained and were re-created long after no one could remember what they truly meant. We pointed the way also with our art and architecture, back to origins on other planets. Origins we had modeled this planet after, or traveled to and from.

It is said that the root of the word alchemy is in this black soil created from the earth and the silt left by the river as it receded from its flooding every year. And the alchemy was born of faith and trust. Every year before the river flooded we were just running out of food again, as it flooded we celebrated its return, and as it receded we prepared the earth and planted, looking forward to yet another harvest.

There was no contract with the nile, no insurance. There was only the faith in some divine source that it would flood every year. There was only its consistency and grace. But when we doubted, we could bring ourselves to its shores, and it would comfort us. Before we built the temples to the gods, we built the temples to honor the river, and the earth, and to be near them. Temples were later built to the goddesses and gods who emulated these natural forces, who embodied their grace, who made even more accessible their power.

There are some temples in Egypt still associated with Oracles of one kind or another, but once upon a time they were in every temple. Beneath the temples that remain in Egypt today, there are often ruins of several if not dozens of other temples before them, just like the layers of other stories within every myth that has lived on into our time. All of these temples were originally built to honor the nature of our origins, and all places, people, and things which stood for that nature. We went there to be one with that nature, especially in the times when it seemed there was nowhere else to go and do so.

Yes, there was a time when even the temples were built for the wrong reasons, or used for purposes far from these described here, but they are not of consequence to us now, except to let them go. The true essence of the universe is not to be found in a temple anyway, but in the heart. Temples were simply built to help lead us there.

The temples were also another way to work with the earth…to surround ourselves with her stones, for they also speak and hold great wisdom. They are the record keepers as well. They still know the stories we sang about when time began, and they always will. The temples were in the stones.

Sometimes there is a sadness that most of us do not still have such temples to visit, but that isn't really true. They exist in the canopies of trees and the singing of crickets. The stones on the beach are no less sacred or telling than the stones we built the temples with so long ago. The sacredness is both inherent, and imbued or strengthened with intention and reverence, as the sacredness in all things is. Some of us long to reconnect with others as we did in the temples. Keep longing. It will come to be.

We are blessed also to have the Ancient Ones with us here in bodies on the earth, in animal form. We all knew that long ago. That is why we honored animals as sacred and associated deities with them. We knew that the animals were the keepers of the gates. Even today, at all the temples in Egypt my beloved Sebastian always showed me where they waited and witnessed, virtually unnoticed by the crowds and the spiritual seekers. The birds that sat in the pillars, and the dogs and cats that wandered their grounds and hovered near their entrances. There stood Isis, Horus, Bastet, and Anubis, alive and unseen.

If you look into an animal's eyes you can see everything. The universe will unfold before you if you truly take the time to notice it. They are the bodhisattvas who have stayed and who have come back again and again to guide and support us, and yet most people consider them secondary at best to human life. They are our brothers and sisters.

The plants speak as well. Just as they have spoken to Shaman, both female and male, for many thousands of years. They have intelligence, and they can let us know how to use them to heal ourselves. They are each so unique and they speak to us with their beauty, their colors, and the design of their life force flowing through them. The woods and the valleys, the mountains and the meadows are alive with voices. This is what the faeries are to me, the beauteous expressions and embodiments of the nature beings. When you talk to nature you are befriending them too, and if you are friends with the land, then the protector deities of that place are also your friends. The support and guidance become exponential.

When we cannot remember why we are powerful or pure, we can look to nature. We can just turn our faces up at night and look at the stars. Nature retains the innocence we so often forget is our heritage, and fear we have lost. When it is not peaceful it can also reflect cruelty and the illusion of randomness. The nature I speak of is how it began, as life in utmost respect of itself.

Innocence is a returning to our most natural state. It is free of assumption and lives within possibility, as we do when at our most authentic. Innocence frees us of the heavy burdens most of us come to know so well in this world, and speaks to us of a place within ourselves untouched by illusion, sadness, or pain. Innocence allows us to be playful, and playfulness allows us to be brilliant.

There are places in this world that are so beautiful to me, that at the mere sight or thought of them I am entirely freed. I become full of peace just knowing these places exist. They remind me that everything I have faith in must be, indeed, real, because nothing of that beauty could have been created by a force that does not know perfection in all things.

Nature can restore our trust, heal us, and give us the space to expand again when we have contracted around the life inside of us. When we give ourselves the moment to close our eyes in the wind, run our fingers through the ocean, lay our bodies down on the earth and gaze into the infinite sky, we can be at one again. All the things in our lives that we need guidance on can come into a different perspective. There is nothing to resist.

Nature, or sense of place, is one of the quickest ways to replenish and to return to a sense of home, reflection, and sup-port. Before we can tap deeply into intuition, we want to refill our inner ocean, and have a nourished basis from which to gain clarity. When our energy is not as low there is less interference, and when we drink from the cup of nature it will always be pure, sweet, and clean.

Gnosis

The Dimension of Feeling

In any thought, object, person, feeling, or action there are many dimensions. We live in a world that operates, for the most part, at the surface. That is why we finally turn to poetry and art in a sometimes desperate attempt to go deeper, when the surface no longer satisfies the innate need to dive into those most profound waters of being. That is why many people are drawn to dramatic movies, because the power, passion, and depth have been edited out of their lives, and while these movies won't replace that, they will simulate a richer experience or wider spectrum of feeling.

We become numb in this world and much of what is modern either supports or creates this numbness. We are brought up as a product of this culture which asks us to stop feeling. We are told, either literally or subtly, that if we feel too much it will only hurt, and draw us away from what we must do in order to live. We are taught to be tough, to hide our feelings because

they would only expose or betray us. Many of us are taught to
look at things at face value, and often only to look deeper if
we think we may be cheated or are searching for ulterior mo-
tives. We are taught to distrust, not only others, but our very
own feelings.

One of the problems with this is that the emotions have intelligence, and are indeed much more powerful than thoughts.
We can think affirming thoughts all day, but it is the *feeling*
we are actually looking to effect. The other problem with this
numbness, along with the subduing of emotion which lessens
our range of experience, is that there is even more to feeling
than emotion. Feeling is our most pure sense. Feeling can tell
us what our eyes, ears, nose, taste, or touch never could. Those
senses are simply embellishments, (though absolutely incredible ones I must say,) to the sense of feeling. The five senses can
open the door to feeling, and they can also bring us pleasure,
one of the long-forgotten reasons we are alive. We have come
to think that life is about suffering. It is supposed to be about
pleasure, suffering being a chapter in the book of pleasure in
life, rather than the other way around.

It is amazing what we build up over feeling...whole cit-
ies. We pave and pave and pave, but the feeling always resides
underneath, slipping through the cracks and causing earthquakes
in our well-structured worlds of thought and protection. It is not
feeling that will hurt us, and if we really reconnect with feeling
it will guide us through all the obstacles that would. Trying to
obliterate feeling will only cause us more pain. Even those of us

who are very open, loving, and sensitive may still have many more dimensions of feeling to be aware of that were shut down somewhere along the way, and that have many riches to give us.

In a sense I could express my whole understanding of intuition in this one chapter on feeling. Perhaps even this one paragraph. You see, the entire secret of going as deeply as you would like to into the intuitive realms is in feeling. In re-membering how to feel, and going deeper and deeper into the experience of it.

For example, perhaps you are unsure about a person in your life and what is going on in your relationship with them. Next time you talk or see that person, notice what you feel when you are with them, and then what you feel afterwards. Are you drained when you hang up the phone? Are you always looking down on yourself when you are with that person, or do you feel honored and understood? I know that some of that has to do with your relationship to your-self, but when we are simply choosing positive or negative influences in our lives, all we have to do is check in and notice whether we feel positive or negative about it.

Perhaps you are planning a trip and can't decide whether to go one place or another…imagine going to each one and notice or write down what you feel. If you don't know the places well enough then find pictures of them or talk to someone you know who has been there, then again just notice what you feel. Compare the feelings and decide which one makes you "light up" more. Then just choose that one.

I know sometimes there are other factors involved in a decision, and those can always be added to the process, but feeling can be like the North Star or the lighthouse which allows us to always have a strong guidepost and focus. We are afraid to trust our own feelings. We often think that is not enough. We think it is too simple or too ephemeral, even inconsequential. Especially when we have been needing to make choices for a long time based entirely on what is practical rather than what feels good. It can be a hard habit to break but let me assure you, it does break, and when the practical and the pleasureful finally meet on the beach for a dance, suddenly everything in life seems to come together. Sometimes we just have to take the leaps of faith before it all makes sense.

We often decide that our feelings are untrustworthy simply because we are so rusty at getting in touch with them. Sometimes it takes practice to reconnect with them before we get a more solid sense of foundation. Often we want to hear it from somebody else, or wait for an angel or being to write it in stars across the sky, or get a professional opinion, or hold back until we have rational reasons for everything. Anything to avoid just feeling, and trusting those feelings. It isn't that there aren't good times to seek these kinds of advice, sometimes they are just exactly the kind of insight or support that is needed to help us spread our wings, it is just about the blessing of knowing that we also have the choice to enter the dimension of our own feelings as well.

Sometimes we think that our own feelings aren't important enough to pay attention to. We think only of everyone else's. This is where trust comes in again. We have to trust that ignoring our own feelings is not going to allow us to take any better care of others, and certainly not of ourselves, and that whatever truth we may find in our own hearts will be best for all concerned from the universal perspective. For example, if someone is hurt by something we choose, without intention of causing harm, then we must know that there is a greater reason. If we hold back our hearts, our joy, our dreams, or our feelings we are not doing justice to life, to god, to ourselves, to anything.

It is never too late to start feeling and dreaming again. It is never too late to decide that whatever happened in the past as a result of not feeling, or whatever number of years has gone by, you have now. And you can start now.

True feeling is like the voice of our intuition. Essentially they are one. When we haven't listened to our inner voice for a long time it sounds distant and watery, and we can't really make out the words when it finally speaks. If we are making an important decision we certainly don't want to trust a voice we can't even understand. The voices of rationality and fear pipe up right away, loud and clear with something to share. They tell us what makes sense, (which as we all know is not always the right thing, just the predictable one,) and what we

shouldn't do again because it caused us pain in the past.
Awfully limited.

What we have to do is be very patient, committed, and
consistent with the inner voice for a while. We have to be
willing, when the voices of rationality and fear quiet down, to
postpone our decision long enough to lean in very close to the
inner voice, and listen, as we would listen to a very small child.
At first we still may not understand its words, but over time
as we pay attention, it will become clearer and louder. Soon
it will be just as loud as the other voices, and we will be able
to understand what it is telling us just as clearly. Then it will
become even louder than those voices, so that we can still hear
them and honor whatever they want to offer, but the intuitive
voice is now the primary response within us. Finally it becomes
our own voice, and the default way in which we function in the
world, rationality and fear becoming purely back-up input, as
they were meant to be. They have their places of importance in
our life experience, just not behind the driver's seat.

Feeling is what allows a person to know which of three
cups turned upside-down might have the berry under it. Yes, it
may take time and practice, but as you become aware of more
and more subtle flows of energy, you begin to be able to sense
the vibrations of things you usually would not have.

That is what attention to feeling produces in us: awareness of the subtle worlds. When we become aware of the
subtle energies we can follow them into deeper dimensions of

understanding. Like seeing the echoes of energy, we can trace our way back to the origins of anything, and see its evolution as well. We can also, more simply, tell which food or supplement is right for us or not, or whether a person is meant to be our mate or not.

Yes, sometimes the emotions override the feeling. That is why we must become artists of feeling, so that we can tell the difference. Yes, life is dynamic and ever-changing and what we read in one moment will be different in the next. That is why we want to keep feeling things anew in each moment, so we are always up to date on how life has moved and what may have shifted.

Feeling is what allows us to read things. Really, we can read into anything we like, within honorable bounds and intentions. We can read a message in the face of a friend or in the leaves of a tree. We can find our fortune in a spread of cards, the palm of a hand, the tea leaves in our cup, or the way the sticks are sitting about our feet in the woods. We can read it in the shape of the clouds, or the skyline of a city. First we have to know how to feel again, and then the signs are all around us and we have only to ask.

When we feel, we become aware of patterns, shapes, colors, gestures, and their possible significances. We begin to see these patterns in all things, and become familiar with flows of energy. At the same time we remain in awe of their endless variety and the spontaneity of life. Everything speaks to us.

However, if we are listening well it is not an endless cacophony of energies, it is something we can tap into and tune into, or not. It is our choice in terms of how deeply we would like to feel into things at any given moment. It is by our will that we choose.

Will and its meaning seem to get complicated or diluted sometimes in our language or understanding. Our will is, most simply, our wish, desire, or choice. Having a healthy will is feeling that we are free to choose, and perhaps being aware of what we desire. Will, like power, is innate to our beingness and is not something we can truly lose or have to earn in specific ways. We can misuse will, just as power can be misused, but we are never without it, and can always learn new ways to utilize it. When we are in touch with our feelings our will becomes clear, and in that case it is always one with divine will, because it comes from the heart.

Gnosis describes the belief that the heart contains all answers, and can provide them for us if we but learn to go within, if we but learn to listen to it. The state of Gnosis is the state of direct revelation from and communion with the divine, by way of connecting with one's inner divinity. Through Gnosis, one becomes enlightened in a way once suggested by the Oracle at Delphi, then spread by Socrates, which is to "Know Thyself."

Sometimes the idea of truly knowing ourselves is daunting, but when we simplify it, the truth is that it is as easy as getting to know ourselves better, the way we would get to know a new friend. As we continue this journey of knowing ourselves, it simply becomes richer and richer. And there is no better or easier way to begin to know ourselves than to get in touch with what we feel again.

It seems simple enough, but as we try to discover how we truly feel about things through the various moments of our lives, we become aware of the layers of conditioning we have received about how and what it is okay to feel. As we begin to unmask this conditioning, we become free of it. Enormous amounts of energy open up as we realize that we no longer need to create two streams of being—our true self and the one we thought we had to create to be accepted.

Life becomes one flow, through which we are expressing our true selves in all situations, and at all times. Then, if there are areas in our lives where it is impossible to be authentic, they cease to be. We are forced to let them go, or leave them behind. At that point, the other opportunities and people that have been on hold can enter our lives, because we have created the space for them.

During my time in India I took a train ride for a few days, and one afternoon I found myself leaning out the open train car door, feeling the immense air rushing by, and watching the fields and trees pass by in amber light. So many messages came to me then. One was that you never have to turn your gaze from god, or the sense of your true nature. If you turn your attention from it to accomplish something else, then you are just distracted, having been drawn out of your center to attain something. Instead, the wisdom told me, keep your gaze on god and your desire and movement toward it clear, and all that is meant to come into your life will enter into that path.

When we begin to "tune in" to what we are feeling, we begin to tune in to ourselves. In doing so we get to know ourselves, and enter the intuitive state of Gnosis, where all is revealed by way of one's own heart.

Ritual

Purification and Empowerment

The roots of ritual are in the spontaneous expression and wisdom of the soul. Ritual was never meant to become something hard and rigid, but to remain mutable and creative. In our day, a polarity has been born between the hardened interpretation and the phenomenon of naturally occurring ritual in our everyday lives. These two ways are meant to go hand in hand.

You see, we experience ritual every day. Some of it with more consciousness or pleasure, other of it simply routine. We can ritualize routine. For instance it is routine to bathe ourselves, but ritual to plan an extravagantly long bath with fragrance or salts. It is routine, perhaps, to take business trips, and ritual to go on a vision quest or to find a new experience, adventure or understanding. It is routine to have coffee in the morning, ritual to drink it slowly by the window and reflect on our lives. It is routine to say I love you to someone we care for,

it is ritual to look into that person's eyes and say it with meaning. It is routine to go to a dance or yoga class, but ritual to
get lost in movement or come into union with the body. It is
routine to have sex, ritual to make love.

Rituals can be made of any situations to which we give
meaning, and as they are ritualized they are enhanced and
strengthened. When we give meaning to something, we are
giving it our energy by way of focusing attention on it, thus
generating power. Repetition and consistency can amplify this
power even further.

Most of all, ritual serves to remind us of something…a
deeper truth about ourselves and our lives. It is a string we tie
around a finger, or an image we hang on the wall that helps to
remind us of who we truly are, and what matters to us.

This is how certain rituals that have been carried down
through many ages or generations became so dogmatized. It
began because one person, or a group of people, either spontaneously discovered or channeled a particular type of experience.
Because this experience proved powerful or healing to those
involved, it was recorded or remembered, and then repeated.
Some of these rituals have kept their original power to this day,
and others have lost some of that power in translation or time.

Either form of discovering ritual can be immensely re-
inforcing for remembering our essential nature or getting in
touch with our intuition. Learning ancient or already practiced

rituals can provide us a wonderful framework and sense of tradition. If a particular ritual feels good and right to us, we can know that it has for many others, in that it has lived on and been passed on from its inception.

The other way to engage in ritual is to invent or intuitively receive the experience. Sometimes these rituals just find their own way into our lives, without the need to invent them. For instance in the examples I used of enjoying a cup of coffee or tea, dancing, lovemaking, a long bath.

There are millions of ways to find joy in our daily lives. We enter into ritual whenever we allow ourselves to deeply experience something. We can also ritualize an experience by repeating it daily or weekly. Meeting with friends may seem like more of a ritual if it were to happen once a week and had a meaningful theme. Lighting a candle might seem more like a ritual if you had chosen the color or fragrance for its significance, and if you were to say a prayer while lighting it.

As we consciously ritualize our daily life, before long everything begins to feel sacred. Reverence assists us in revealing the hidden meaning in all things. As we discover the power of ritual, we exercise the faculties that allow us to hear the voice of the universe speaking to us in every situation.

We find rituals in our lives through indulging in what brings us joy or the experience of healing. If dance class is what we love and look forward to every week, then that is something we can ritualize, and give even more meaning to. Or it could be something we add to other rituals we create. It is what we are naturally drawn to that inspires ritual.

Another way that inspired ritualization can enter our lives is through direct intuition or revelation. As we become closer to our guides, they may have some suggestions of certain rituals that could serve to empower us or offer purification and clearing. Similarly, we may simply feel drawn to do something that we usually don't in our daily lives, as a special activity that gives new meaning to, or symbolizes something we are working with. Like making art, once we are comfortable with the tools, we can just allow ourselves to create.

For the most part, we have lost the sense of ritual in our culture. We are left with holidays and the very few rights of passage that still remain. These can be ritualized as deeply as we would like to make them, but for many of us are not enough to encompass our desire to utilize ceremony. These events include holidays like christmas, easter, and halloween, all of which have pagan origins. The rights of passage include things like school graduations, marriages, retirements, divorces, births and funerals.

The ritual itself is not always the actual agent for healing or change, but a way to honor or acknowledge a shift that has already happened, thereby enhancing or empowering its occurrence or results. Often its representation will symbolize the actual event, as a way to bring the experience more into conscious view or awareness. For instance, when we know we are letting go of certain things in our lives and we build a fire, write words that express them on a piece of paper, and then burn it. In that way we also use ritual to enhance and expand our intention, bringing things more powerfully into being or completion.

Even the most simple of ceremonies serve to amplify intention or its results. Simple acts such as the paper in the fire I mentioned above, or cutting a ribbon or string as a symbol of ending a negative connection with someone. They empower the life experience by creating a physical embodiment of its energies. How we choose to embellish the moment is entirely our choice and directed by what moves us. Maybe it is meaningful to us to be in nature, maybe it is setting up an altar or lighting candles, maybe it is having or making music or sound to go along with the experience.

Simple rituals, which may also be incredibly deep, are a wonderful way to honor new beginnings or accomplishments. Honoring what is new in our lives is a beautiful approach to setting intentions, and to acknowledge how far we have come in bringing this new thing, or event into being. It is a way to celebrate, and as we strengthen our relationship with celebration, we make more space for joy.

Ritual is also a powerful tool for honoring our dreams and desires. Often we do not have the support for our dreams that we would wish to, and it is easy to get caught up in the inertia of that negativity or lack. When we do a ritual in the name of our dreams, it is like adding coins to a piggy bank or money to savings, it creates an energy resource that builds up to support us in accomplishing that which we want to. A ritual for our dreams might be creating a collage of images which represent our hopes or goals, or writing them down and placing them on an altar, or speaking each dream into a wild flower and casting them into the ocean. Sometimes adding release to your desire is the best possible way to allow something to come into being.

Gratitude is an emotion that will often spontaneously inspire us to create ritual. When we feel gratitude naturally or authentically, rather than feeling that we have to impose it falsely, there is an impulse to express it. Like the true desire to say thank you when someone pays you an amazingly beautiful compliment, or hug someone if they give you an incredible gift you would never have expected. It is a reflex to give back when someone or something has given to you.

This is how reverence truly originated, out of gratitude for answered prayers or gifts of the earth or from others. For example, when a place of natural beauty overwhelms our senses with color, fragrance, and feeling, we may instinctually want to sing a song, dance, or paint an image in awe of its generous splendor.

Ritual often serves to offer us one or both of two energies: purification and empowerment. Purification is not related to making us more pure than we already are, but to restoring our innate and eternal purity, and removing obscurations to its evidence. Therefore, in a way, to purify something is to return it to its pure state, thereby naturally empowering it. Empower-ment is also a result of returning or helping to bring something to its most natural being or essence. When something is in resonance with its most essential way of being, it is naturally empowered, or imbued with its original strength and lifeforce. So, truly, purification and empowerment imply one another.

Creating something, be it ever-changing or more static, that gives us a sense of ritual in our lives can be like food for the soul, and can draw us even more deeply into the Intuitive Life. Whether it is actually in ceremony, learned or invented, or the ritualization of our joyful habits or hobbies by simply giving them more awareness and frequency. Through ritual we can have a consistent lifeline to our memory of what we hold dearest, what really matters to us, what we most value that is already in our lives, and what we would most like our lives to become.

THE ORACLE WITHIN

Creativity

The Soul of Inspiration

Just as song is a natural extension of speaking, dance a natural extension of movement, and lovemaking a natural extension of love, creativity is a natural extension of the Soul. The Soul, in its most inherent state, is constantly self-expressing its essence. For many of us, creativity and inspiration may already be a mainstay and source of great joy in our lives. For others of us our creativity has been over-criticized, over-compared, or has had to be set aside in pursuit of other goals. In those cases, we find that creativity and inspiration are at a very low level in our lives.

For many people I know who express that they feel depressed, or are suffering with a health condition, depleted energy, or lack of a sense of purpose, it is creativity that brings them back to life. I agree that art, in its limitless forms, can and does save lives. Because the art of the Soul is not limited to painted papers and certified skills. It is as varied as the Souls that may create it. We can make an art of our meals, our prayers, our living spaces, our way of speaking, how we dress, our gardens. The ways that we can make art of our daily lives, along with the ways we can enter into it with special projects or emphasis, are absolutely endless. When we have curbed the Soul's desire to make art, we are stifling life force, and when we encourage the Soul to express and allow life to be its art, it finds its natural state of joy again.

Entering into the world of the Soul's art is the best way I know to discover or rediscover one's sense of purpose, true work or service, or gifts in this world. It is an incredible chance to tap into memories of skills or teachings that the Soul has carried for many ages, many lifetimes, perhaps since its birth into being. This is how creativity brings us back to our source, reminds us of what or where we come from, and helps us to feel more connected to our true nature and the divine.

There are so many ways to feel lost in this world, and also to experience loss...so many ways to feel estranged from ourselves, from others, and from the divine. Creativity can be a lifeline when nothing else makes sense anymore, when it is hard to even have faith or hope, when we feel alone and unable to enjoy the things we once did. In those times even the most therapeutic treatments may not touch or reach us, but if we can find something to give ourselves to, and lose ourselves in creatively, it can become like a boat that carries us to another shore. It can give us the chance to heal, and make something good from our experience of pain and the feeling of separation.

Very few of us are taught or raised to follow our inspiration above all else. If we are taught that inspiration has a place, it is usually with certain conditions or compromises. We are often told that it is like a bonus, but not a requirement in life. Requirements are paying the rent, maintaining the right image, meeting the common standards of "success." We are not usually asked what success would mean to us. For some people success would require fame and earning a huge income. For others, it would mean finding simplicity or love. For some of us success would mean becoming a professional, others would be happy to learn a more modest trade and live by the ocean their whole lives. We are not taught to consider what success would feel like to each of us, or to ask ourselves what role inspiration might play in attaining it.

We may have every luxury, but if we are uninspired, it will mean nothing. We may have nothing, but if we are inspired, we may be able to accomplish whatever we desire. The golden road of our dreams is not built by chance. You must dig up the mud of self-creation, then, in learning to make the bricks from that soil, find that in laying your path with them they turn into gold. The mud of self-creation is not meant to be discovered by way of a hard-won secret or indiscernible treasure map. As we allow ourselves to rediscover what inspires us, we find that it is all around us all the time.

In our world there are often very strict rules about what makes one an "Artist," and if you are not "serious" about it in certain set ways, then you are usually not considered worthy of the title. This is not to take away from the special things we can learn by taking a professional approach to the arts if it is our path, but frequently something is lost about the inherent artistry of the soul...something we never have to learn. Some religions would tell you we were born in sin. I believe we were born in love, and that we were, and are, all born artists. It just takes finding your inspiration so that you can learn what kind of artist you are. Being an artist of the soul can be applied to any profession on the face of this planet, and many more yet to be defined. It is not as much about what you do, but how you do it, and how you feel about doing it.

We so often get lost in drudgery in this world. Our days are consumed with things we really don't want to be doing. We begin to resent life because it is filled with things we dislike, or even hate, but feel obligated to do. It becomes a web, and its stickiness the glue that holds us back from re-igniting. If you have found yourself in one of these webs, it is easy to begin the process of disengaging. Find even one thing that inspires you, in any way, and dive into it as deeply as you can. Perhaps it is just a picture of a far-away country you have always been drawn to. Maybe you start to read about it, then save money for a trip there. Maybe while you are there your life changes, your heart opens and heals in a new way, you make a different choice about what will come next for you.

Maybe you have always been interested in a healing modality. Perhaps you aren't even sure you want to practice it, but you've always wanted to learn it anyway. Remember that your inspiration does not have to be practical. It may become practical in a way you could never have planned or expected, or it may simply lead you down a new path that has many other things to offer. I do believe that life and the divine want to make our dreams and goals attainable in a practical way, it's just that life has a wisdom that we often don't realize it has. If we plan every little thing in a practical way, we may limit our choices and life's ability to make them possible for us in remarkable or miraculous ways.

This, once again, is where trust comes in. To follow your inspiration is to follow your heart, and to follow your heart is to trust. Sure, you may need to keep one foot in the world of the practical so that you feel confident you have the resources to bridge you into your inspiration, I am just suggesting that you think about having one foot out as well. One part of your-self that isn't wing-clipped by fear and that is free to explore the infinite realms of the possible. As this part of us gains strength, it can begin to conduct our sails. It knows how to direct our boats toward the land where the universe can help to practically support what we dream is possible...but first we have to dream.

As we become sensitive to what inspires us, we may discover things we discarded for one reason or another, they didn't seem practical as we have addressed, or perhaps they just seemed downright unattainable. Maybe we decided that we just weren't any good at what we liked, or maybe someone told us that. Maybe we decided someone else was better at it than we were and became intimidated. One thing is for sure. No one can be better than us at something only we ourselves can do. The art of the Soul that each of us makes is absolutely unique, and if you don't make your own Soul's art, no one else can. It is only yours to create.

Maybe we decided our dreams were silly, but if we chose to explore them more deeply by writing or reading about them, looking up classes or workshops or programs for them, we might discover that they were not, or that what we were interested in was a sign post or gateway to something else closely related. When we allow ourselves to fall down the rabbit hole willfully, it is true that we don't know what we will find, which is the source of some of the fear around it, but it is also equally true that whatever we may find on the way, we are headed to wonderland.

Wonder is an entry point to inspiration. We live in a world that frequently crushes wonder into digestible little bits of fact and presumption. Most people pretend to have everything figured out…anything to avoid the ambiguity which the universe is actually constantly existing in. Neat lines are drawn around everything with perfect labels. When you are outside of these shelves and boxes, you instantly irritate people for whom nothing usually is. They quickly put you in whatever box you are closest to, so that their view of life and the universe does not end up in jeopardy. When we allow wonder in, when we don't need to have all the absolutes in a row, magic re-enters the scene. When, instead of registering a flower we have seen a hundred times by name or recognition, we simply allow ourselves to marvel at its beauty and the fact that it grows from a tiny seed, we are giving ourselves the chance to fall in love with life again. There are so many things to be in wonder of, and it is the antidote to the negativity and jadedness we are often surrounded by in this world.

To be in wonder is to see the same thing twice, or even over and over again, without assuming it will remain the same, or have the same meaning. To be in wonder is to experience something more than once and not limit your expectations to the same outcome. To be in wonder is not to fear chance, but to fall in love with it.

Knowledge can easily be liberating or limiting. As long as knowledge continues to be an open-ended step toward more understanding, it is a vehicle for the former. When knowledge becomes a seal we place on something, it closes a lock on the door of wonder, and we are less and less able to enter inspiration. We have to forget what we know sometimes in order to return to the Oracle within, and remember everything.

The word inspiration actually refers to the ability to receive and communicate sacred revelation. There are entire cultures and spiritualities for whom inspiration is still purely understood as an experience of connecting with the divine, and therefore with one's own intuition. For them, inspiration *is* divine, like direct revelation, and thereby an immediate tap into the experience of one's own intuition.

Inspiration brings us home…for in being drawn to create, we are actively reminded that we are creators, and of what we are created from. We return to our most natural, original state, whether we are making a poem, making a toy castle, making a wonderful meal, or making love. We are making something, and that act is divine.

When we are inspired we find enthusiasm, and the root of the word enthusiasm, *enthos*, has been interpreted as meaning "god-filled." As we are filled with our own truest nature, so we become filled with life, healing, and illumination.

The Body

Companion in Bliss

I remember ancient times in which the body was considered the very holiest of vessels, and no search for a grail of any kind, could have been more sacred than the search for the revelation of the body.

To connect with the body was to honor it, celebrate it, make it a work of art either in adornment or in movement. The body was our most intimate expression of god. We honored the sweat and the blood, the breath and the tears as one flowing river of divinity. More than just knowing that the body was not separate from the divine, we felt that our bodies were indeed the proof or evidence of our divinity. That is why, later, religions and governments which sought to control had to defile the body, so as to destroy the power of that clear piece of evidence...so that we would forget we are god.

However, they can never destroy that power, even in the modern attempt to manipulate our bodies through widely advertised standards of beauty, and at the level of our very genetics, there is a force beyond their tampering. It is this force that has always been celebrated in the body by those who remember, and always will be.

In the temples of so many lands, it was the body that was first honored before initiating entry into the other worlds. The body would be ceremonially washed, simply meaning washed with the intention of purification. This purification was not meant to correct the body of impurities in its being, but to honor the body by relieving it of anything non-essential to its nature.

The body was always attended to, its needs heard and met. It was rubbed with herbs and incense, it was anointed with oils, it was painted, it was massaged, it was pampered. Pampering the body was a sign of godliness. Cleanliness was simply one aspect of the worship of the body. It was worshipped because it carried the secrets of all the universe, and because it could always be trusted. It was when we began to distrust our bodies that so much of the Great Forgetting happened.

In one of my warmest memories of my past soul experiences, I was a temple dancer. In my time, we danced to worship the Goddess, and our dance was the dance of creation. It was considered symbolic of the offering of lovemaking to the divine, and therefore representative of the creative force in all things. We enjoyed little more than our bodies, nature, and each other as reasons for, and vehicles for, experiencing the essential bliss of the universe.

We danced to represent the aspects of creation, and the forces of the cosmos. We danced to remember our source and our story. Our hands became birds and flowers, and our hips and chests the oceans and the trees, rolling with the winds, and bending with the weight of ripe fruit. We were the Goddess, and we were God. We were worshipping ourselves, and each other. When the Great Forgetting came, some of the dancing stopped, but it lives on inside each of us and is returning by the day. Whenever we dance, we are once again inside our temple, being held by the divine.

The body is a great friend. At best, it is our vessel and channel for all that we would wish to hold and bring through in this world. And when we are holding or bringing through something we do not truly and deeply wish to, it shows us. It is one of our greatest mirrors, and wisest teachers, and even when we feel at odds with our own very flesh, it is indeed still a temple to our souls.

The body, a network of light, filled with cells like heavenly bodies orbiting our spirits, will follow us until the end, and then it will let us go. It will materialize and manifest what we carry in our light or energy bodies so that we can address these things. It will always attempt to heal and expand to meet whatever we set before it, whatever may be the will of the Soul. Even if it may seem to, due to what we are experiencing in order to learn, it will never, never turn against us.

Sometimes we have repressed what the body has to say for so long that we become afraid to address it. We think things may have gotten too bad, and that to look would only make things worse. The truth is that things are always better than we fear they are, even at their worst, and the sooner things can be looked at, the faster they will heal. Sometimes we don't know where to begin with the body, and all our seeking seems in vain. That is simply when we are working through many layers, and as we continue to search, we will eventually find the gold of illumination and healing. In fact, it is always finding us, we just need to turn our direction toward the light and make sure we are open to receive it.

It is amazing how often the body is ignored on the spiritual quest, or even when included, put in the backseat or in a secondary role. The body is a means for spiritual revelation, and like many other practices or focuses one may hold, can provide the gateway to complete god-self-realization. Once we are no longer afraid of the body, or even nervous about it, then it can become uncharted terrain ready for exploration.

For many of us the body feels unsafe, as if it is the body that exposes us to pain or to harm. For some of us it began when we entered into this world. It may have been physically painful to take a more dense form than the one we had known before. By falling in love with our bodies we can shift our experience of what it means to take form. We can come to know it as a celebration, and a powerful vehicle for the spirit. We can come to know the body as a haven rather than a threat.

For others of us the body has never felt like a threat, but perhaps like a distant relative. We know we are related to it, but we are not close. Maybe there are certain places or situations in which we feel connected to the body, but other times when we completely shut it off. We all know what it feels like to constrict around fear, and to feel our bodies do the same. The goal of remaining connected with the body is not the avoidance of constriction, though it may naturally become less frequent the more comfortable we become with the body, but to simply stay connected to it no matter what it feels…to give it space and permission to feel what it needs to, and to acknowledge it.

It is fascinating to find out that your body holds all the secrets of the universe, and could give you intuitive insight on absolutely any aspect of your life, or the cosmos. It is a process of becoming aware of it, of learning how to listen to it speaking to you. This is how kinesiology or "muscle testing" works. The body already knows the answers. It is built into our biology, our cells, our chemistry, our very bones.

For example, when you think about something in your life you would like guidance on, what does your body do? Bring up an image in your mind's eye of the situation, place, or person, and then pay attention to your body. Does your breathing change? Do your muscles tighten? Does your face contract or expand? Do you smile? Does your chest cave in or open?

Each of the tiniest particles in the universe holds the whole within it. I sometimes practice something I call the

Cell Meditation, in which I visit the cell of a certain object or being…an organ or part of the body in distress, a tree, anything at all, and then I communicate with it about the overall health or wisdom of that object or being. It is simply one more way to ask for information. Sometimes, since we live in a vibrational universe, I ask the cell for a healing tone or song for the body it is a part of, and allow that sound to be sung through my voice.

Some of us are very close to our bodies, and deeply celebratory of them, but may still find that there are doors down lengthy corridors that we haven't opened for a very long time. They hold information, wisdom, and energy, sometimes even memory. They are a part of the knowledge kept by our greatest record-keeper…the body. It has been said that the Soul *is* memory. The Soul is the memory of what we have experienced as unique beings, and that we identify with. The Soul, then, is our unique song in the universe, and to be with the body is to remember that distinct and special vibration, and to remember how to sing it into our lives.

The body holds the memory of this song in a physical way. Many times, when we want to seek intuitive guidance, we sit or lie down and *tune out* the body in order to go inward, out into space, or into the imaginal realms. This is what holds some of us back—because we haven't heard the body first, and it may have many things to say. Those things can create a kind of static or interference on the line, not to mention block the body-wisdom that might arise.

I often recommend an easy sound and body-mind awareness practice to use before attempting to access intuition. It is very simple. Begin by noticing what you are feeling, both physically and non-physically. It helps to say it out loud. For instance, in scanning your body you may notice a soreness or tightness that you hadn't been aware of before. Similarly, scanning your thoughts and emotions, you may realize that something is still bothering you, or on your mind, that you didn't realize. Sometimes we don't really check in with ourselves for days, or weeks, or even longer.

Then just breathe into what you are feeling. It doesn't matter how many times. Then, allow sound to come out. Absolutely any kind of sound, for as short or long a time as you like. The most important thing is never to force the sound, simply to *allow* it to come from what you are feeling. Then breathe again. And when you are ready, just notice what you are feeling again. It is phenomenal what such a simple exercise can do. It is not a prayer for world peace, it is not sent intentionally to heal something inside of you, in fact you may even be in a very hard or desperate place when you do it, and yet it has the power to create aspects or effects of both.

It is often when we are most emotional or desperate that we need guidance, and that it is hardest to have the clarity to find it, but when we let the cork out and relieve the pressure of all the unexpressed feelings that have been building up inside of us, we suddenly find the clear and still place from which to see very far.

Another simple but wonderful way to allow the body to briefly express before attempting to reach intuition, is to simply stand up and shake off first. Yes, you could certainly put on some music and dance around the room instead, which is another fantastic way to experience the body, but sometimes we are not in the mood to dance or have little time and very much want to tune in for guidance anyway. Just standing up and allowing the body to hang, shake, or move a little, can really do wonders to release what may be on the surface of your consciousness. Then the body and the mind become friends and servants of the intuition, working in harmony with the heart's desire.

More than anything, the body wants to be loved. It wants to be adored in fact. It mirrors you in that way too. It wants to be nurtured and experienced and explored, and it wants to open. It wants to feel intensely, even when you don't. It wants to feel special and appreciated. It wants to feel deserving of utter reverence. You can start by trying to see yourself and the way you look physically in a new light. You can start by telling yourself you are beautiful, because even if you don't believe it at first, if you keep telling yourself, you eventually will. This is because somewhere inside you know that it is true, that you are right, that you are beautiful...and that you can still be anything you want to be.

The body will not resist us if we surrender to it. It will always look for and find ways to open to us more deeply its secrets, and its answers, and its gifts. Our body is often the greatest

untapped treasure trove and resource of pure energy that we
have access to. As we begin to give it our attention, it naturally
releases more and more of this energy to our use, along with
the intuitive information to tell us how best to use it. With this
blessed and magical combination, we find the fuel and the fire
to change our lives, and to make of them what we will.

THE ORACLE WITHIN

Beings

Support and Guidance

In my world it isn't such a big deal talking to beings. It isn't something coveted for the special few, nor something strange for the rare eccentric soul. Talking to beings is something we all know how to do and have done thousands, if not countless times before. In fact, you and I are beings, no different in essence than Isis or Shiva, the Mother Mary, or Quan Yin. We are all made of the same feathers, and gold dust, and stars.

I often say I simply have some friends with bodies and some friends without bodies. We all have both kinds, many of us have just lost touch with the latter. The lovely part is that they never lose touch, however, with us. Beings which serve as our Guides, those not embodied, be they Deities or Angels, Ascended Masters or Faeries, Animal Spirits or Elementals, Relatives or Friends, Goddesses or Gods, are all part of one Great Family of which we are a part. Their reputations or associations only mask the fact that they are just like us, and we are one of them. More than that in fact, we are one *with* them.

And these beings, our guides, adore one thing more than all else, and that is to serve the divine by extending and express-ing their absolute love to us. The beings that serve as our guides do not serve with mixed intentions or reasons. They are simply overflowing with gratitude for the revelation of the beauty and love we are all made of, and sharing it with us is like being able to write and sing a song about it, or to create never-ending ecstatic poetry. They live for the joy of expressing it, and the joy of its reflection in our opening.

Beings are available to us twenty-four hours a day. They don't get tired of holding a phone to their ear, or mind being disturbed at 2 am. They don't run out of energy. They don't mind if our questions for them are small, and seemingly insig-nificant or mundane, or huge, serious and deeply meaningful. They say that asking them the mundane or simple questions in our lives allows us to find the guidance that frees us from giving those issues power, so that we can instead place our energy where we would like to.

Oftentimes it is the little things that take up the full stage in our minds and daily lives, and this is why the beings find them as important to us as the more obvious issues on our spiritual path. I have frequently found that it is a misconcep-tion that beings don't know much about how to be practical or physical, since most of the ones I know have been both, though there certainly are some that substantiate that claim. I have found that most of our guides do understand what we go through or face in the physical, because even the physical is still made up of energy, and both readable and discernable for them.

One of the first steps in becoming able to connect with your guides is allowing yourself to be at the same level they are. Those who have attained enlightenment simply have a different vantage point from which to remind you of your true power and beauty. We often imagine beings as huge or distant, a far-off illumination. I always suggest that you begin to imagine them as your size, near to you, and then even as if they were a good friend you were about to have coffee with, and talk to about your life.

It is like the difference between talking to an acquaintance and an intimate friend. You would share things about your life in two totally different ways with one and the other, and have completely different comfort levels. To begin to see beings as good friends, it is first important to find or think of some that you have already felt a connection to. Maybe you have never actually been able to see or contact them, but have always felt moved or compelled when you've seen a statue or altar card of their image. You don't have to wait for someone to tell you clairvoyantly that this being could be one of your guides, you simply know it because you feel it.

When you have picked a particular being you feel connected to, in some cases it may be a group of beings, then begin to imagine that being in a friendly way, as if you were already close and this being already knew you and loved you well. Imagine a comfortable and lovely setting, and then bring yourself to that place to meet with that being. If you are unclear on how the being looks, you can literally ask the being to help you see her, him, or it more clearly, or for the being to show itself in a way you can identify or relate to it. Beings are happy to show themselves in whatever way most suits your connection to or recognition of them. They are also happy to assist you in hearing their voices more easily or removing any interference.

In fact, sometimes beings just give you energy when you meet with them, rather than words of guidance or messages. Sometimes it is all unsaid, but by communing with them energetically, all the answers are somehow understood or come to you soon after. It is not important how we see or communicate with beings so much as that we call on them frequently. This is because when we call on beings, whether by name or simply by making an inner request for them to draw near, they are able to more easily and powerfully offer us energy and support. Since energy flows where awareness goes, when you place your awareness with them, your whole system—body, mind, heart, and soul, open and receive more.

Never doubt that your prayers are heard. They may not be answered when or how you expect them to be, but never doubt that they are being listened to and worked on by a team of angels and beings at every moment. Your prayers are golden and deeply sacred. The wants and desires of your heart are a holy scripture to the divine, because the heart is divine and what it truly yearns for is of inestimable worth.

When I was little, one of the things I held sacred was a little box of "worry dolls," which date back to an ancient Native American tradition. The dolls were tiny little creatures the size of an almond at most, made of wire and paper, with painted faces and small cloth coverings. There were girl dolls and boys, each a little bit different than the other because they were made by hand. To use the dolls, you were supposed to take them out of the box before bed and give each of them one of your worries to work on during the night, and then place them under your pillow. This way your worries were taken care of and you could sleep in peace.

This is a beautiful illustration of what beings can do for us. We are taught that this life and even the journey of the soul are about work, and striving, and earning your worth, but it is a myth and a terrible lie. You must *know* your worth, and never try to earn it. This life, and the journey of the soul, are about learning how to play...about learning how to let go of burdens as quickly as they come to us, and never being fooled by them. Yes, beings come to love us and guide us, and, essentially, those are just the means to the end of helping us become lighter.

Our Guides want to help us find the White Heart. The heart that when weighed against a feather on the great scales of the Goddess Maat, is lighter. The ancient Egyptians believed that if, when we died, our hearts were as light as the feather on those great scales, we would pass through and gain entry to the Blessed Lands…lands just like the ones here on earth but without any of the suffering. Our homelands.

However, it is not just when we die that this process happens, it is in life. Every day, every moment, our heart is weighed, and if it is heavy we remain amongst the suffering, and if it is light we remain in the Blessed Lands. The beings, our Guides, want to assist us in retaining the White Heart, so that we may be in our homeland, always.

Perhaps someone in our lives is causing us pain, maybe willfully, or maybe without even meaning to. Perhaps we have lost our sense of purpose, or just can't find the inspiration for it underneath our daily worries. Maybe we are preoccupied with tax problems, the dental care we really should get, a job we don't know how to move on from, or an obligation that is weighing us down. These are all things beings can be of assistance with, either with words or energetic support.

There are many ways to talk to beings. If you find yourself having trouble doing so, try the simple sound exercise or movement I described for releasing surface energies. Then attempt to commune with your beings again and see if you notice a difference. Try writing down your experiences every time you reach out to your beings, keeping a journal of what happens during each encounter.

Perhaps it is a time in your life that you just don't feel you can make that connection, or you haven't ever done it before and don't know how. It is no less important, and in certain cases even more supportive or confirming, if you make the connection with your guides through a medium, channel or intuitive. Just make sure to filter it through your own intuition to see if it all resonates and feels right to you, remembering that intuitives are also interpreters and that your own interpretation is most important.

Wherever you get your guidance or communion with beings, it is valuable. Finding your own ways that work for you, and therefore having whatever access you can to this support is what is important. For at its root, that is what it is all about in communicating with beings...*support*. As we talked about on the subject of trust, the more support you have, the easier it is to fly free in the skies of your own true nature.

Sometimes trust issues are the main barrier to receiving this support, and rather than judging the trust issues, it is important to honor them. We want to feel safe reaching out to beings or the other worlds, just as we want to feel safe with a person when opening our hearts to them. Feeling safe sometimes gets an undue bad reputation. Fearlessness is the state in which we are born as souls, however that fearlessness was born from a place of feeling total safety. It is not about waiting until everything feels safe to move forward, but about having the willingness, courage, and desire to move through fear in order to find that safety on the other side. We find fearlessness when we have walked through so many of our fears that there simply aren't any left.

To find a sense of safety and protection I recommend using what I call the "buddy system" with beings. You begin by finding a being you know you can resonate with and recognize, a being that feels deeply close to your heart. Establish that connection first and become familiar with that connection. Then, if you decide you want to approach other beings or travel other worlds more extensively, you can always call on the being that is your "buddy" if you get into a position in which you are unsure or afraid. Like the feeling I had holding Chapala's hand during the Durga Puja that night in India.

I also like the method of imagining your guides at the four corners of your house, your room, your bed at night, or even gathered closely around your body if you feel the need for the remembrance of protection very deeply.

When you know you can call on a powerful being for refuge, you are like a child with a flashlight in the dark who knows that she or he has a finger on the button and can create light when and if ever they need to. For me protection is just like that light. There are many wonderful tools and practices that we can use to support ourselves and to remember that it is there, but in essence we are always protected. It is like an immune system. It can weaken under certain conditions, but only with purpose and when we attend to it again it becomes strong once more. I also think of our protection like the ruby slippers Dorothy wore…they were always with her but until she knew how to use them she did not know she had the power to get home. Like what it takes to build self-esteem, or the feather that convinced Dumbo he could fly, we just need a reason to believe.

We can learn to use our powers of self-protection by experiencing the ways that beings protect and support us. It is like being held up in the water while you are learning to swim, or having training wheels on your bike until you can find balance on your own. Sometimes we haven't needed the training wheels for a long time, but don't know it until we take a ride without them and see that we are fine. Reflection is what reminds us of who we are, for when we forget we may cease to be it. Beings lovingly hold up a mirror when our arms are too tired to lift one, or when it is too hard to find one in the haze of this world.

Usually when a client comes to me for a personal session, their guides wait quietly until we have begun the opening sound and discussion afterwards, but sometimes they present themselves right away, very excitedly. They are so thrilled that this person they love so much has come to someone who can speak their messages out loud, and sing their healing songs. They are so glad for a physical vessel and assistant for the work they do from another world. This is what the best of the Shamans and Oracles, Priestesses and Priests have done since time began. "The best" not by some form of unidentified merit, but in clarity of intention, that true food of the gods.

I talk to beings almost every day. It is as much a part of my day as eating and sleeping. And when I forget, and get caught up in something that strains my heart or uses too much of the energy of my mind, I am always so relieved to remember that they are there for me as a resource and support. It is amazing how easy it is to forget, but when you do consistently remember that you can find help and answers, your life changes radically. You stop feeling lost, or in despair, or torn with confusion. You may desire more human friends, but you never feel truly alone unless you wish to be. You stop being unsure about how to make your dreams happen, because whatever length of time it may take, there is always guidance on how to make steps forward when you feel stuck along your way.

When I met my guides, as I told the story of earlier, it changed my relationship to all beings, and my life, so deeply. I had been able to see beings since childhood, but never had they seemed as such friends to me, like family. My guides opened a gateway for me to feel closer to many, many others, and remember my connections with them.

Our Guides can also remind us of our past lives, and the gifts from those lifetimes or soul experiences, because they knew us then as well. There are lifetimes that we have worked very closely with them, and they can tell us many stories about ourselves. Like family, they can remember us from long, long ago, and help us to remember ourselves.

They know our ancient selves, for they are the Ancient Ones, and so are we. They remind us of this truth. All beings have an aspect of themselves that is the Ancient One. When beings come as the Ancient Ones, I know they are coming in their most primordial form...the form they held before they were known as Isis, as Tara, as Magdalen, as Yeshua. Before they led a human life or engaged with humans in a way that led them to a particular name or identity, they already existed as an Ancient One, and still do.

Most of the beings I engage with have led human lives at least once. They believe that telling their stories creates healing for people, because we can find our reflection in them. This is how myths began, and why sacred scriptures were originally written...to preserve these healing stories. I have found over and over again, in direct contact with these beings, that their stories are often different from what has been passed down as myth. In some cases the power has remained in the stories, and in others time and intentional manipulation have altered them to remove most of the healing essence—though even then it is still there, if you read carefully enough between the lines and draw your own conclusions. And just as Isis has her healing stories, you have yours that you can pass on to others. You also are a Goddess, a God, one whose stories are full of the power of love and loss, pain and redemption. Yours, too, can help others know how to return to themselves. Sharing with beings, and hearing their stories either by myth or direct contact, can help us discover this.

We are all channels. Every day, every moment, we decide what we want to channel. We can channel our true selves, or one of the many aspects of the self we wear as fronts in this world. We can channel our creativity, or our insecurity. We can channel the celestial. We can channel nature. We can channel the wisdom of a friend or being. We can channel what we have been fed, without asking ourselves if it is what we believe. We can channel hate. We are all open vessels. The journey is one of becoming aware of what we are open to, and deciding whether we want to be. As we become aware, we have the power of choice.

The universe is already in love with you, and has been for all time. In fact, the universe loves us so much that expressions of this love can be found everywhere, if we can but remember how to see them amidst all the persuasive distractions. Beings and guides are messengers of this love. That is how you will know any beings that are unfavorable or not advanced enough to be a guide, because they would not be messengers of that love. Among the beings that are your true guides and friends, the love is so potent that it overwhelms the cells with joy and light. Even great Goddess Kali, wearing her necklace of skulls, is wrathful in the name of love. And the demon-god Mahakala, devours evil and darkness in the name of love. Just as these beings can seem or act harsh in the name of love, so can love always manifest in whatever form it needs to in order to liberate or defend us.

It is love that drives the hearts of these divine beings, just as, when we are at our most aligned, it is love that drives our hearts. We are loved in a way that I will never be able to tell you in these words alone. We are loved the way that we have always wanted to be loved, and that many of us may feel we never have been. We are each an invaluable jewel, adored and watched over with the tenderness and consciousness of that which made the stars and the endless sunsets, the rolling ocean and the rustling leaves. We are loved forever, and if beings can embody this for us, we are one step closer to knowing it as an eternal truth.

THE ORACLE WITHIN

Hold not that which you see as dark within you. It is of myth and not of truth. Hold not that which you see as imperfect within you. It fades in the luminosity of your greater beauty.

Know that the lighted path is yours. Even if the light comes by firefly.

My heart extends to yours...I am at your call.

In Love, Isis

THE ORACLE WITHIN

Sound and Vibration

The Song of the Soul

Right now you are singing a song. In fact you are always singing one. It changes, though the essential melody remains the same. The core vibrations are sustained as the basis for the ongoing tune. But it becomes softer, then louder, richer, then simpler. New melodies or instruments come and go. The mood changes, the texture. And it is beautiful, so beautiful, that the angels are in love with its radiance.

It is the natural vibration of your heart. It is the signature your soul came into being with. It sounds like a song and it is made up of your intentions, your dreams, your memories, and your gifts. Other people can hear it, but they don't know that they can. It is simply what draws them to you or repels them. Just as you feel the songs of others and respond similarly. Sometimes you may even be drawn to someone simply because there is a vibration in their song that you know you have, but have forgotten how to sing...and you want to remember.

Sometimes our song becomes dampened by negative thoughts about ourselves or life, or by the energetic residue of difficult experiences. This is when it is most important for us to clear these energies, and we do so by having our song reflected to us, and therefore renewed. We may experience this through the pure song of nature, or the presence of a good friend or guide, through our creativity, or through a sound healer who, at her or his best, is in the work of reflecting, re-tuning, and restoring the songs of the soul. We can also, as I will describe, be our own sound healers.

For each of us is born, lives, and dies with a heritage of sound. Vibration is our essence and our birthright. It is what we are made up of, and what we make up of life. It is how we create, and have been created. Sound refers to audible vibration. All the other kinds of vibration are inaudible to the human ear, but still audible to the soul.

You see, everything in the universe, both formed and unformed, has a vibration. This is how it exists uniquely. Physics tells us that all matter is constantly vibrating, and that it is this which gives matter shape and allows it to hold form. This is one of the reasons why sound and vibration are such powerful vehicles for *changing* form, since they are its building blocks. Sound allows form to change and become new form. Sound reduces a thing to its most essential element, vibration, and then gives it the chance to re-design from there. In this way conscious sound is naturally clearing, and inherently empowering.

Even healing without sound is vibrational healing. This is because intention itself has vibration. All will and directed energies have vibration. The chair you are sitting on is vibrating, just at a slower rate or frequency than the cells in your body or the light in the room. That which is more dense vibrates more slowly. Sound is denser than the higher, inaudible vibrations, but less dense than the body. This is what makes it such an excellent bridge between the worlds of spirit and matter, as it has been used by almost all peoples from every part of the world, as far back as history has yet to discover.

Sound is used over and over again to create trance, to assist Shamans, Medicine People, Priestesses, Priests, and Oracles in healing, and to ease the communication between our world and the spirit world. Knowing how to use sound intentionally to heal, to have a more clear connection to your intuition and guides, or to consciously create your life, is to live a lucid life. A lucid life is one in which we become aware that it is we who are dreaming the dream, and have the power to become conscious of it and change it at will. It is to become aware that we are the creators, as we are one with god.

It doesn't take years of training, though that may enhance or enlighten the experience. In fact, babies know about sound healing. They know how to make sound to release emotion, whether through a giggle, murmuring, or a scream. Animals know about sound healing. They know how to moan when they roll on the earth on their backs, or whine when they are in need. In essence, they know how to express themselves through sound and that is the first step to understanding how to use it to heal or reach new states of awareness.

In our world to be an adult is to polish one's words to the point of exhaustion, almost until it doesn't matter where they come from, only how they sound. Meaning becomes lost, and communication becomes performance. To allow our words to be real, and our sounds to be authentic, is a powerfully altering process. That, too, is sound healing. Long before we may learn what toning is, or have a repertoire of mantras, if we can just remember what our own soul sounds like, we are already using sound as a deeply healing tool.

Sometimes it is the more identifiable aspects of sound healing, however, that give us that gift. For instance, sometimes it is getting lost in the rhythm of a drum, body and mind, that brings us to this memory of the soul. Sometimes it is learning that by extending a sigh we are toning, and by allowing these tones to come forward, we are altering our consciousness and even our physical form. Sometimes it is by learning a particular mantra, which holds the power and assistance of a specific deity or aspect of self that brings us to oneness. For some of us it is a pop song or any piece of music that speaks to us or touches something in our hearts. What we come to love about sound or vibration will be unique to each of us, but knowing about their possibilities gives us yet another tool for living the Intuitive Life, and therefore more consciously remembering the true nature of our souls.

The key or secret to understanding the healing and re-storative powers of sound and vibration is intention. Without intention, sound is just a wave of energy. With poor intention, it is a negative wave of energy. The same song, sung by two different people, could have two completely different effects. One may not make us feel much at all, or even agitate or upset us, while the other may make us cry, laugh, or feel greatly moved. It is the passion and presence behind the sound that decides its potency or outward effects.

I am a singer. And though I manifest this in obvious ways, each of us is one, whether we record and perform it for others or share it only with our gardens and our private spaces. I have found the relationship with the voice to be one of the richest and most powerful I've ever experienced. For me, there is no other instrument as intimately tied to intention as the voice. I often say that there is a great reason why nearly all of us on the planet are born with one, and even those who are not able to speak have a voice, and find the other ways to express it. For we are using our voice even when we silently make art, or write, or gesture. The voice is larger than the vocal chords. The voice is the expression of who we are, and even when our words say one thing, the voice may reveal something different. Most people have forgotten how to listen to the voice. They only listen to the words.

When we come to truly own and embody our voice, a thousand birds are set free into the night somewhere inside of us. It doesn't matter if we have been told we are a bad singer, or think our voice somehow otherwise not beautiful. Beauty is an unnamable creature, and the real beauty of any voice is in its opening and authentic release. Nobody can teach you that, though they may be able to help illuminate the path. Only your own soul can show you and give you that gift. That gift simply wants to be romanced, nurtured, and adored in order to fully open. It too starts with self-love.

When we begin to allow our voice to match our feelings, we are set free and our power, if concealed, returns to us in full glory. We stop being afraid to speak the truth of what we feel and think, and our life starts to match more clearly our inner world. Again, in that way, sound becomes the bridge. For there is an Ancient Voice, inside each of us, that we begin to align with as we reclaim the one we have in this world. And it is this Ancient Voice that knows the answers to all things, is the inner voice of our intuition, and the voice of the heart.

For the heart is always speaking to us. Whether we choose to follow thoughts or fears instead, whether we trust the word of others more than we do it, or whether we think guidance only comes from great beings, it always speaks to us. I know that the trouble is sometimes in knowing which is the voice of the heart, and how to hear it clearly. When we align our expressive voice with our feelings, we open a more clear channel for the voice of the heart to be heard.

Beings can be of great assistance in reminding us or in helping us to hear what the voice of our own heart is saying.

They can help to affirm or confirm for us that we are hearing it clearly. They can also offer us assistance or healing through sound. Certainly they may sing through a sound healer who is also a medium or channel, but they can also sing through you. Just call on a particular being, deity, natural element or animal spirit and then ask them to share their song, allowing it to come through your own voice.

Sometimes having a crystal bowl or some kind of resonant instrument while you allow yourself to make sound can be very supportive. It is by no means a requirement for getting in touch with your voice, or your guidance, or the divine, but sometimes it mirrors the support we have from the universe by making an underlying tone or background sound for you to resonate with or build upon. In so many ancient cultures sound was shared communally, in groups. This is something we can experience in sound circles or even more traditional gatherings like choirs or jam sessions, musical plays or by being a part of a band or performance group, but when we do not have these opportunities or wish to explore sound privately, an instrument can offer us a sense of communion. Sometimes there are places we can only go with ourselves or when surrounded by like-minded or similarly intentioned others.

We can also feel this communion, as I mentioned before, by sharing with beings. When we can sing with Quan Yin and be a vessel for her song of compassion, we are likely to feel anything but alone! When we can tune into the songs of the whales or dolphins and allow the sounds we feel from them to flow through us, we are likely to feel very nourished, and as if we are among friends, or even families. We are likely to feel resonance.

To resonate with something is to be able to vibrate at the same rate, or to naturally be in tune with it. To harmonize with something is to vibrate at a different tone or rate, but one which creates a harmonic or harmonious effect. Harmonics are infinitely occurring overtones which take place simultaneously with any sound, and are considered to be inherently healing. Most overtones are inaudible, however certain instruments such as Tibetan bowls, didgeridoos, dolphin songs, and the human voice, can make audible harmonic sounds. Dissonance, on the other hand, has been shown to have distressing or damaging effects.

When we resonate or harmonize with something, it is a reflection of the way in which we are vibrating, which can either be a wake-up call or a supportive encouragement. The places we go, the people we know, the things we like to do, they all have their own vibration, and when we engage with them we match it. That is why we want to be conscious about the situations and people we choose to involve ourselves with and make sure they match what we would most like to be experiencing in this life.

We are alive with movement and song. It is a greatly empowering realization to know that we can decide how we would like to sing the song of our Soul, and that we express it with the choices we make in our lives, and by what we align our vibration with.

When we can stay at home in the true song of our souls we don't feel swayed by the other vibrations around us, and can more easily maintain and embody our authentic essence.

Then our song becomes a symphony, a hymn, an un-self-conscious melody that pours out from the deepest and holiest place in our souls…and when others walk by, hearing something familiar, they turn their heads to the sky, and smile. They are hearing the music of the spheres, and you have become a vessel for the sounds of the infinite love of the universe.

THE ORACLE WITHIN

Joan of Arc

My fire,
They say it causes pain.
My fire,
They say it isn't right.

My fire,
They say it's made of stars.
My fire,
They say it gives off light.

Like Joan of Arc,
Burning for what I've done.
Like Joan of Arc,
Burning for everyone.

In a world,
Where we run,
From the fire inside,
We're afraid to shine,
And so we learn how to hide.

Because we know,
If we are light,
Then we will fall in love with ourselves again.
We know,
If we are light,
Then we will fall in love with ourselves again.

Like Joan of Arc,
Burning for what we've done.
Like Joan of Arc,
Burning for everyone.

So, in a world where when faced,
With fire, most turn,
I spend my time,
In search of the ones who burn.

Who, like Joan and me,
When we were down to the wire,
Found that hell, isn't bad,
It's just heaven, on fire.

Song By:
Jennifer Luna Posada

Passion and Risk

Flame in the Heart

We are born of passion, the passion of a universe that explodes into sparks and then flame, heaves in the seas in waves, brings each of us skin to skin, sends blood pumping through our bodies and hearts, and bursts into birdsong, and lightning, and rain. And in this universe which loves itself enough to make you and me, the closest thing I have found to realizing that we are that creator, is to discover we have nothing to lose.

I know it doesn't seem that way. And indeed the grief we can experience by way of loss in this life is beyond words, but to know truly that there is no such thing as loss in the universe is the exit from the maze of suffering that sets you forever free. To know that energy is never destroyed, only transformed, and that all things you have experienced before can be attained or experienced again beyond this world, is deeply liberating. And it makes a friend of something most of us avoid…risk.

Risk is something we usually fear, because we associate it with potential loss. When we are not afraid to lose, then risk becomes a gateway. Like any gateway, we still want to be extremely choosy about which we select. We don't want to gamble on something we don't even care about, because then risk is simply self-destruction. That is where passion helps us. Through it, risk becomes chance, and chance becomes opportunity, and opportunity becomes freedom.

Passion is our true North Star. It is what will open the mysteries of the universe to us, and it is what will let us know that which is hidden beneath our deepest layer. It is what will tell us the truth when everything else seems to lie or hide. When the mind is full of rational perception, when the body is numbed, when the words are a veil, true passion will speak for the heart.

For true passion is not the same as convoluted attractions and desires, it is the desires and attractions of the Soul. Sometimes we learn to avoid these, not just because we are taught that they are not practical in this world, but because we are so afraid that the weight of the beauty will crush us, that the deepest longings of our hearts are too strong a swell to contain, and that they will decimate somehow our entire reality with their power. We believe the animal within us will take over.

But it is not the animal within that we fear, it is that our will would not be strong enough to channel it in alignment with our truest intentions. It is not the great serpent that we hold back at the base of the spine, or the lion waiting in our hearts. It is not the mighty bird whose wings sprout from our backs, or the wolf that begs us to speak to the moon. It is our own fear that we are not strong enough to know our power. It is our own fear that if we truly knew who we are, we would cease to lead a normal life, or be able to communicate with others, or continue daily function.

It is our knowledge that we are wild at heart that causes most of our culture to put everything in neatly labeled containers, to isolate emotion and to shelve the elements we are born of—our water, our fire.

We are taught that our fire burns, and that it will ravage homes, friends, countrysides. We are taught that there will be damage if we let our light shine, and the fault and responsibility will be ours. We are taught that our light is too bright and will blind those who look at us. We cover, we conceal, we let little bits shine when we feel safe and then apologize for it if blamed or shamed later.

There are few things worse than shame. Shame, in one of its many forms, is often the greatest reason that we close off our light, bury it under the earth within us, eclipse its glow. Maybe someone once told us that it was not all right to be a beautiful soul and to know it. Not okay to trust yourself more than anyone or anything else. Not okay to find your temple within, and to adore the idol only of the Self, in its countless forms, on the shrine of the body, and the altar of the heart.

It doesn't matter so much how you say the words you choose in a prayer. It is the passion with which you make or recite it. It is the passion you invest, passion indeed being your very life force, that makes miracles happen. It is your finest asset and the greatest vehicle for extending the gift of god within you that I have ever known. For indeed, its extended form, compassion, is one of the most revered approaches to embodying the divine. Com-Passion. With Passion.

If we really believe that there is just this moment, and that it contains all moments that have been or will be, why not take a chance? Why not trust? Why not have faith? Why not dream bigger, be bolder, open more, remember hope, learn something new, throw out what you don't need, love deeper, embrace longer, enjoy more richly, treat yourself...love yourself?

What is there to lose? Nothing but that which is false to your true nature, if the passion for your true nature becomes your reason for living. For your true nature is love, and what greater reason for living is there?

If some things move out of your life, do you doubt or fear that they would not be replaced with those even more suited to you, even more fitting and perfect? With trust there is always the knowledge that even the roughness has riches to give you later, that even the pressure and the hard black coal have a diamond meant to be yours.

The senior quote I chose for my yearbook when graduating high school, written by an anonymous author, was,

"The sublimity of wisdom is to do those things living, which would be desired when dying."

It comes back to that wonderful practice of asking yourself, "If I were to have only a few years left to live, what would I do with my time?" And that, my dear friends, is just the beginning. That is just the moment when the curtain opens to the truest form of your living. Then, there are worlds upon worlds of adventure and joy...new things to love and be loved by, new horizons and new colors and new dimensions. And these are the things we think only come when we get to heaven. Not true. These things are indeed very enjoyable in heaven, but we are also meant to be able to enjoy them here and now. Heaven was never supposed to be something we had to wait for, or earn entry into. Heaven is our home and our essence. Heaven is where we belong, and are welcomed and loved always.

Hell is simply the experience of feeling separate from ourselves, and therefore from the divine, and the sin which takes us to hell is purely doing that which is against our nature. The more deeply we betray our own nature, the more painful the "hell" of suffering feels to us. And yet, heaven waits for us, even when we do not know it.

To do those things living which would be desired when dying, is to realize we are alive. It seems simple and yet it is so profound to fully embrace living. When we feel alive, and feel our aliveness, we naturally experience gratitude for this ability simply to *be*. For the chance to experience passion, and to pursue it. A flower blooms inside of us that never dies, and whose fragrance is the drink of the soul. Staring down into the waters of our passion, we find Forever, and that we are always held gently in these great hands. We discover a red rose at the center of our being that knows everything about our passion, and opens every door to bring it into life.

Two Black Doves

There was a story told at the site of the Oracles of Dodona in Greece. It was said that the place was deemed sacred by the arrival of a bird...a black dove.

Two Priestesses of Ancient Thebes in Egypt, now modern-day Luxor, had been abducted by slave-traders and thieves, and in order to free themselves, they had transformed into two black doves, and flown away.

They chose black in honor of the Void...the great darkness from which all things come. They were powerful women, for they did not fear their own darkness...knowing it was simply that which is unrevealed. They knew it was a part of the great night-sky body of the Goddess Nut, and therefore also contained stars.

They flew in two different directions. One flew to the site of the Temple of the Oracle at the Siwa Oasis in what is now Libya. The other flew to Dodona, Greece, and it is said that she landed on a tree branch and began to speak. Some said that she could be understood, and others that she spoke in a foreign tongue, but for both she was marvelous, captivating the hearts of those who witnessed her. She was the one who founded the site, and who taught Priestesses to hear the messages in the sound of the wind through the Oak Trees. This is why the Priestesses at Dodona were called peleiades...doves.

At Siwa, the other Priestess anchored the legacy through the underground waters, spreading the message and the memory to farther reaches of what was then considered part of one land, Egypt. She created this temple to her own standards, and dedicated it to the god Amon, the Hidden One.

Like the two Priestesses, like winged Isis, Horus, and Maat, we too can take flight and liberate ourselves in the alchemy of the black doves, and, like them, we can spread the memory and the message of our true heritage throughout the world. We must, for in doing so we restore magic to its rightful place, and sow the seeds of the Great Remembering forever.

The Return of the Oracle

I was born to write this book. And I have written it many times before. It has been burned, buried, hidden, and lost. It has carried the light of illumination that I hold in my soul, and that you hold in yours. There is something different about this time however. This time that I write this book I do not do so in hiding, or in the express interest of only a few. This time I write it at the dawn of the Great Remembering, and nothing can change the turning of the tide. It is done.

Several years ago it was proved at last by science that indeed a fault line, two in fact, ran under the temple of Apollo where the famed Oracle of Delphi gave her prophecies. For the first time since the original excavators deemed the stories of the gaseous fissure in the earth to be untrue, science began to validate the stories of the Oracles again. However that is just one of thousands of still tiny fissures of a new kind. These fissures are in the veil of the Forgetting and they are letting in the light of the Great Remembering of who we truly are. I believe that discoveries like these are a sign that the time of the Oracles is returning, and that they will return in numbers. And to do as they have always done…to remind us.

It is time dear sisters and brothers, the light of the dawn is here and we may rise again in that sweet light, and tell the things we know until that light is lit in the others' eyes, and in this way passed throughout the earth. I believe that those who refuse to remember will have a different path. Theirs is also blessed, but for those of us who are ready to remember there is a new earth to dream into being, and this time we know how we want it to be.

Never give up hope, for I too believe that the day is returning when the beings walk among us as friends and the galaxies open to our calling and the earth speaks to us through the trees and the mountains and the waters again. For some of us she has never stopped. We have been the keepers of the song, the original song we were born singing, the love song of the universe. The truest music of the spheres. And we must not let the song go now just because things sometimes look bleak. We must not be distracted or believe in the illusions that dance around us like the temptations of the Buddha. We must find the North Star within us and stay true to its course. We must find reasons to believe and be inspired and to allow that inspiration to flow from us. For inspiration moves faster than the speed of light, and far faster than nega-tivity or fear. We just have to believe. Without belief, love and faith are robbed of their natural powers and become meaning-less concepts adrift in a sea of doubt.

We can start by believing in ourselves, along whatever path thus far described calls us the most. We can start anywhere, with the smallest of steps. We start with what we feel passionate about, then we must simply let the passion guide us into the holy of holies of our hearts. Then we let the passion, the compassion, become our reason, and our strength.

Seek reflection my friends. When your candle goes out look for the people, the places, or things that relight the flame. Drink in the natural support and nurturing that is available to you through creativity, companionship, your guides, or nature. Know that there is more than enough to go around, and that you can have more than enough. Know plenty. First get to know plenty by visiting her in the world of nature, and then she will come to visit you and enter your life endlessly. Find the nuggets of gold that are hiding in the places you didn't expect or haven't looked. See how life is conspiring to make your dreams come true and to show you what a fascinatingly beautiful creature you are. Throw away your masks, unless you need them for a fantastic masquerade party.

Remember what lightens and gladdens your heart, what inspires you to play or to open and trust. Laugh and cry, and get on your knees, and dance. Remember what you dreamed about before you decided you could not have it. Find out what it is like to fully feel again. Get angry, get excited, get free. Don't compare yourself to anyone and give more compliments, and know how to tell someone off if they are trying to make you smaller.

Offer shame to the fire of your unparalleled brilliance and light. Find your own true song, which no one else can sing, and belt it to the world, or hum it comfortingly to yourself at all times. Be your own best friend if there is any way you can. Write, think, dream, live and love as fully as you are able. Retreat, nurture, and fill yourself with peace and silence if you wish. You are unlimited and potential is your companion forever. Nothing dies, it just changes shape.

Give yourself permission to set yourself free of the things that hold you back. You know what they are and you owe them nothing. Get off the wheel of karma and into the ocean of trust. Turn heads, be invisible, dress up, go naked, follow whatever calls your heart. As you do, others will begin to hear the song within themselves just by being around you. You become a part of something again and the organism that is the universe lives through you, around you, and within you, and time stops and you just *are*.

You are a butterfly and it doesn't matter how long you were in the cocoon or how long it took you to get out. It doesn't matter who you thought you were before you knew yourself. It only matters that you are radiating color and flight now, that you are alive and this is a new moment and it is yours.

I am looking over at an image of Isis I brought from Egypt. It is a plaster mold of a temple relief. There is a layer of turquoise paint in the creases, and she is smiling at me now. We have a secret, the one that you know now and have always known. The one that is written in this book, the one that the Oracles know. This is her book, and mine, and yours. It belongs to us because it is our story, and our legacy, and our soul. We are born of the infinite, and in the infinite we exist forever. Oh, keepers of the flame light the way for others, and in re-igniting their flames watch the world burst into light. Give to your heart what it asks for, there is no better way to please the Goddess than this.

Tread upon the ground of your fears until they become your good friends and there are no enemies left. Call upon the ancient heart within you to be your guide. It has seen all and knows all. As you do this you are the Oracle who returns, and the promise of the Great Remembering is complete. And the day that we all prayed for as we closed our eyes to sleep, has come.

THE ORACLE WITHIN

Jennifer's Sound Healing CD
Soul Sounds:

Oracle, sound healer, channel, writer and lecturer, Jennifer Posada takes us on a journey of pure sacred sound and bliss.

In her voice the deities of the inner realm find a place to express a timeless message: that we are all creators of ultimate beauty and joy.

Jennifer opens our hearts so we can receive the blessings of those who guide our paths upon this Earth, inviting our souls to celebrate the radiant essence of our existence.

"If these songs offer a sense of loving comfort, I am greatly honored and fulfilled. If they offer the sense of being guided and held, I am overjoyed. And if they give you just a glimpse of the amazing star that you are, I am ecstatic. The gifts that I have been given are gifts that each of us have to offer in our own unique way. We are all oracles, angels and artists. Here is to the special light that shines only from you."

— Jennifer Luna Posada

Soul Sounds may be purchased online at *www.jenniferposada.com* or by calling us at 360-376-1062.

Jennifer's Writing

To access archives of Jennifer's writing online, to purchase more copies of this book, or to stay tuned for future publications, visit: *www.jenniferposada.com*

Jennifer's Workshops

Jennifer offers multiple workshops throughout the year based on ancient alchemies and the process of exploring the Oracle Within. For a complete schedule visit: *www.jenniferposada.com/workshops*

Ordering and Contact Information:

To order more copies of this book or other of Jennifer Posada's products, either visit *www.jenniferposada.com* online or contact our office:

Jennifer Posada
P.O. Box 1715 Eastsound, WA 98245
jennifer@jenniferposada.com
360-376-1062

Printed in the United States
65103LVS00007B/221